TABLE OF CONTENTS

Unless otherwise indicated, all Scripture quotations are taken from the *King James Version* of the Bible.

31 Secrets for Career Success
ISBN 1-56394-042-6
Copyright © 1998 by *MIKE MURDOCK*
All publishing rights belong exclusively to Wisdom International
Published by The Wisdom Center
P. O. Box 99 • Denton, Texas 76202 · 1-888-WISDOM-1 (1-888-947-3661)
Website: www.thewisdomcenter.cc

❦ Psalm 19:11 ❦

"Thy word have I hid in mine heart, that
I might not sin against Thee."

———❖———

≈ 1 ≈

LISTEN TO TAPES OF THE BIBLE DAILY.

———————▶➤◉◀———————

Listening Is Different Than Reading.

You cannot read and do other things at the same time. Reading requires total focus. You have to move away from everything else that you are doing.

However, listening can happen the moment you wake up in the morning. This is powerful.

While you are washing your face, *you can receive the words of Jesus* into your spirit.

While you are shaving, taking a bath or making up your bed, you can receive His Words into the soil of your mind. Most of us take an hour or so to birth our day. That is 60 minutes that the holy Words of God could be *washing your mind.*

His Word *cleanses* (John 15:3).

His Word *energizes* (Psalm 119:149,156).

His Word is *life* (John 6:63).

His Word *purges and purifies* (Psalm 119:9).

His Word *corrects* (2 Timothy 3:16).

His Word *warns* (Psalm 119:11).

His Word *brings peace* (Psalm 119:165).

His Word *births an invisible joy* that cannot be explained by anyone (John 15:11).

Here is what has happened in my own life. Sometimes, I become so busy, I delay taking my Bible and reading quietly in my Secret Place. I explained to the Lord that I would meet with Him later, "when I can really concentrate and not be distracted by anything else." (This procrastination has cost me dearly.)

Listening to Scriptures on cassette tapes solves that problem *immediately.* Satan can throw many things at you, but the Word of God is *still washing* your mind, because of your daily habit of listening. However, listening is not a substitution for reading. You need both.

Reading affects your *thinking.*

Listening affects your *feelings.*

Reading affects your *mind.*

Listening influences your *emotions.*

His Word always creates marvelous results, regardless of how you receive them into your spirit. But I have found that keeping tapes with me in motel rooms, next to my bed and in my automobile really influences me.

Keep tapes in your car. They will discourage boring conversationalists who talk about trivia and other unimportant things. Also, it makes it possible to hear His Word away from the clutter of business and home chores.

Keep tapes next to your bed. Sometimes, when I'm having difficulty sleeping, I will punch "play" on my cassette recorder and listen to the Scriptures. Words cannot describe how instantly an atmosphere and climate can change in your bedroom when the Word of God fills up every corner!

Keep tapes on your desk at work. Using your headphones, you will always find an opportunity to receive His Word into your spirit.

You will change in direct proportion to the Words you are hearing from Him.

Your joy will be proportionate to the Words you are hearing from Him.

Nobody else can do this for you. You must pursue the Word of God for yourself. *Today.*

Somebody has said that it takes 56 hours to read the entire Bible through. Whatever it takes, do it. Do it today. Concentrate on developing this habit.

His Word is the most important thing you will hear today. *It will change you forever.*

This is *One of the Golden Secrets to Career Success.*

≈ John 7:28 ≈

"Then cried Jesus in the temple as He taught, saying, Ye both know Me, and ye know whence I am: and I am not come of Myself, but He that sent Me is true, whom ye know not."

～ 2 ～

Pursue Qualified Mentors.

Mentors Are The Easiest Way To Learn.
Your Mentor will unlock your greatness.
Mentors are more than teachers.
Teachers love *information*.
Mentors love *protégés*.
Teachers enjoy *education*.
Mentors enjoy *impartation*.
Teachers study to *know*.
Mentors study to *sow*.
Mentors are not necessarily cheerleaders. They are coaches. Their role is not merely to confirm what you are doing correctly. Their goal is to *correct* you and prevent you from making a mistake.
There are 2 ways to learn:
1)   Mistakes, or
2)   Mentors.

5 Facts About Mentorship

1.   *You Will Usually Have More Than One Mentor In Your Life.* Financial, spiritual, and academic Mentors exist everywhere.
2.   *Different Kinds Of Mentorships Exist.* Some of us are mentored through tapes, books and

relationship. However, there can always be a primary Mentor who remains with you throughout your life.

My father is the most important Mentor in my daily life. For many years I struggled to impress him rather than receive from him. I wanted him to celebrate my discoveries rather than sit and absorb his own discoveries. After understanding mentorship, now I learn more from him in a single day than I used to learn in a year. Pursue, cherish and protect your gift from God, your mentor.

3. *Respect And Protect The Access Your Mentor Permits You.* He will not always be there. You must face some battles alone. So drink deeply from his well now while you have *access*.

4. *Treasure Any Invitation For Private Discussion With Your Mentor.* The presence of others changes the level of intimacy and information. When I am alone with my father, I receive much more than I do when others are present. The information is more specific. Exact. Precise. *Just for me.* The thoughts and opinions of others present often dilute and even weaken the impartation.

5. *Your Mentor Often Discerns Whether You Discern His Worth Or Not.* No words need to be spoken. Flattering words are unnecessary. Persuasive words do not matter. When you are in the presence of someone who truly respects what you know, you detect it instantly.

Pursue Qualified Mentors.

That's One of the Secrets of Career Success.

≈ 3 ≈

Negotiate Everything.

Nothing Is Ever As It First Appears.

I walked into a luggage store here in Dallas many years ago. When I had selected the luggage I desired, I asked the young lady if she could provide a "corporate discount."

"What is a corporate discount?"

"Forty percent off."

"All right!" was her reply.

With one simple question, I saved several hundred dollars. *Negotiate everything.*

While standing at the airline counter, I was informed that my excess baggage was over $200.

"I was hoping you would show me a little mercy today," I joked gently.

The agent thought for a few moments and replied, "All right." With one simple statement, I saved over $200.

Negotiate everything. Your words are creating financial gain or loss.

Your words are bringing Increase or Decrease.

Your words are creating Doors or Walls.

Your words are Bridges or Barricades.

The Scriptures teach it:

"A man shall eat good by the fruit of his mouth" (Proverbs 13:2). "The wicked is snared by the transgression of his lips: but the just shall come out of trouble" (Proverbs 12:13).

Here Are 10 Facts You Should Remember When You Want To Negotiate Successfully

1. *Attend Negotiation Seminars, Listen To Tapes, And Secure The Counsel Of Qualified Mentors Before Doing Any Serious Negotiation.*

2. *Successful Negotiation Requires The Right Attitude.* Nobody wants to be taken lightly, intimidated or pushed. Everybody is involved. The lady in the luggage store wanted to sell the luggage, create favor and a happy customer. I gave her *the information* which would accommodate that need, a forty percent discount. (I later returned to buy many other items because of the favor she showed.)

The airline that graciously permitted me the excess baggage has become my favorite airline receiving over $100,000 of my business each year.

Negotiation must be viewed as a win-win situation for everybody involved.

3. *Successful Negotiation Requires An Understanding Of The Cost Involved For Others.* Donald Trump explained why his father was so successful in negotiating prices. His father invested time in finding out exactly what the cost was for those he was negotiating with. This enabled him to know exactly how far to negotiate.

4. *Successful Negotiation Requires Proper Timing.* Many years ago, I was very weary when I arrived home from a meeting. The flight was tiresome. As I walked into the office, a staff member

approached me.

"I've got to talk to you!"

"All right. Sit down. How can I help you?"

She was very aggressive and flippant. "I need a raise!"

"Well, how much are you wanting me to increase your salary each month?" I asked.

"I need a $1,000 a month raise."

I almost laughed. I really thought she was joking. She wasn't. She continued, "My husband and I are moving into a new home that we have just built, and I really need the income to pay for the house."

It was so ridiculous to me, I almost laughed aloud. But, I proceeded to advise her *gently* that, perhaps, it would be well for her to find another job where she could secure the salary she needed. I asked, "Your present salary was created by a list of problems you chose to solve for me. Now you want a huge increase in salary. Do you have a list of the new problems you will begin to solve for me?"

It had never crossed her mind to solve more problems for her new salary.

5. *Successful Negotiation Involves Long-Term Gain, Not Short-Term Gain.*

The famous billionaire, Sam Walton, said he never invested in a company for where it would be in 18 months. He invested in companies that would succeed ten years down the road. An employee can often squeeze out an extra dollar from a boss during a crisis situation. But if it creates a wall of separation, that staff person can cause a deeper problem in the long term.

6. *Successful Negotiation Requires Quality Time.* Don't rush anything. You will never do well in something that has not taken thoughtfulness, sufficient time to collect information and necessary data. Run from the salesman who insists that "this is the last day of this sale." Don't fall for it. When you return a month later, they will still deal! They need your purchase more than they need their own product.

7. *Listen Longer To The Needs Of Others.* Listeners are rare. You are developing an understanding of the concerns, fears and passion of the hearts of those at the negotiating table. Wisdom is worth any price. Invest the time to listen thoroughly, compassionately and expectantly.

8. *Successful Negotiation Should Focus On Details That Truly Matter.* Several years ago, an impressive young couple wrote me about a job. They were making $5.00 an hour. He was riding a motorcycle to a second job. He had three children and worked sixteen hours a day on two jobs at $10 an hour total. They were destitute. My heart went out to them. They had driven all night to meet me face-to-face for an interview. I agreed to pay him what both of his jobs were presently providing for working 16 hours a day. Then, as a gesture of caring, I included their housing if they would do additional yard work at my home. They were thrilled and elated. Over a period of time, I purchased furniture, dishes, clothes and so forth. They were enjoyable, so I was happy to do so.

Soon, someone must have inspired them to negotiate for more. Every opportunity to "squeeze me," such as appliance breakdowns, they pushed. I noticed a pattern. It became one-sided.

When you have many employees, you cannot give everybody a raise when you desire to. You can't always give it to them the moment they deserve it. *You have to think long-term for the organization.* Something within me became agitated. So when the oven broke down, they wanted me to replace it. I was weary of replacing everything. I requested that they pay half, and I would pay the other half. They attempted to use harsh words to negotiate with me. I'm not the kind that responds well to intimidation.

I realized they were frustrated. So I explained that they had 45 days to go find a new house, and they could purchase it themselves. Yes, they were good people, but were poor at negotiation. They lost a wonderful blessing trying to squeeze "an extra nickel." Don't lose dollars trying to save pennies.

9. *Close Doors Gently.* If you realize that you have to end a relationship, close doors quietly. You may have to return through them again in the coming years.

10. *Never Burn Bridges Behind You.* Everybody talks. Everything you do is being discussed by many you have not yet met. Don't schedule unnecessary conflicts in your future.

Yes, I agree, your opinion deserves to be heard.

But make certain that it is heard at the right *time* in the right environment and with the right *attitude.*

Negotiate Everything.

It's One of the Secrets of Career Success.

➽ Mark 6:31 ➽

"And He [Jesus] said unto them, Come ye yourselves apart into a desert place, and rest a while:"

————➤•◦•◄————

≈ 4 ≈

Never Make An Important Decision When You Are Tired.

Tired Eyes Rarely See A Great Future.

When I am weary, I am not the same person. I don't have the same kind of faith, the same kind of enthusiasm and the same kind of patience as I do when I am rested, strengthened and feeling good in my spirit.

Fatigue Creates 10 Potential Mistakes

1. *Fatigue Makes Mountains Look Bigger.* I don't understand it. But it's true. When you are tired at night, things that normally would appear simple suddenly feel very burdensome and complex to you. Tasks that usually require a minimal effort suddenly seem too much to take on.

2. *Fatigue Causes Valleys To Seem Deeper.* Discouraging factors seem to enlarge. Disappointments seem keener and stronger when your body is worn out.

3. *Fatigue Causes Offenses To Come Easier.* You will seem more offended than you normally would be. Little things become big.

When you are tired, your mind replays wrongs

that people have done to you.

When you are rested, your mind moves to positive, wonderful and glorious dreams. Things you want to accomplish and do.

But fatigue will affect you in the opposite manner.

Jesus understood this. That's why He encouraged His disciples to "come ye apart and rest awhile" (read Mark 6:31). One of our great U.S. Presidents once said that he would never make a decision past 3:00 in the afternoon. He was too tired and weary to consider every option available.

4. *Fatigue Makes You Less Tolerant Of The Views And Needs Of Others.* When others are weary, they seem less understanding of your own opinions and views, also.

5. *Fatigue Makes You Focus More On What You Want Instead Of The Appropriate Method For Achieving It.*

6. *Fatigue Turns Your Focus To Short-Term Goals Rather Than Long-Term Goals.*

7. *Fatigue Causes Your Conversations To Be Filled With Rash, Hasty And Unusually Inappropriate Words.*

8. *Fatigue Makes You Become Unwilling To Invest Appropriate And Sufficient Time For Planning Ahead On A Project.*

9. *Fatigue Causes You To Meditate On Your Own Mistakes.* In the ancient writings, there is a reference to satan wearing out the saints. I believe it. "And he shall speak great words against the most High, and shall wear out the saints of the most High," (Daniel 7:25a). Preoccupation with your own flaws

can be exhausting and eventually even devastating.

10. *Fatigue Can Birth Any Obsession With The Flaws And Mistakes Of Others.* Then, you begin to blame them for everything that goes wrong.

Rest restores.

Never make important decisions unless you are strengthened, mentally alert and spiritually perceptive.

That's One of the Secrets of Career Success.

≈ Matthew 12:37 ≈

"By thy words thou shalt be justified, and by thy words thou shalt be condemned."

❧ 5 ❧

USE EVERY CONVERSATION AS A PRACTICE MOMENT FOR IMPROVING YOUR SPEECH.

Make Your Words Count.

Here Are 7 Facts You Should Remember In Every Conversation

1. *Avoid Sloppy Casual Conversation.* Pronounce your words *clearly.* Enunciate every single phrase to the best of your ability. Each conversation you enter is a practice session for excellence. It's too late to work on excellence when you walk onto a public platform. "By thy words thou shalt be justified, and by thy words thou shalt be condemned" (Matthew 12:37).

2. *Never Speak When Another Person Is Talking.* It takes away from the value of your own words. If someone interrupts you while you're speaking, don't insist on being heard. Rather, say nothing. Permit them to speak. Then, dominate your turf.

3. *Qualify Others Before Speaking The*

Secrets Of Your Heart. Withhold your opinion until someone who values it shows up. "A word fitly spoken is like apples of gold in pictures of silver" (Proverbs 25:11).

4. *Speak Loud Enough For Others To Hear Clearly What You Are Saying.* Don't mumble.

5. *Never Assume Others Have Understood What You Have Said.* Sometimes, people are thinking about many other things while you are talking. Their mind is *not* on your words. They can be nodding in total agreement with your words, while their thoughts are a thousand miles away.

6. *Encourage Others To Speak Clearly.* When others mutter or mumble, speak aloud, and say, "I did not understand. Please repeat your words."

7. *Always Invest The Necessary Time In Searching For The Right Word,* Even In The Midst Of A Conversation. *Right* words are worth the time involved in finding them. *Wrong* words are devastating enough to avoid.

Making your words count *in every conversation* will increase your skills dramatically.

48 Facts About Words

1. *Words Can Poison And Destroy A Young Man's Entire Life* (read Proverbs 7).

2. *Right Advice Guaranteed Safety And Protection.* "In the multitude of counsellors, there is safety" (read Proverbs 11:14).

3. *Any Man Who Controls His Mouth Is Literally Protecting His Own Life.* "He that keepeth his mouth keepeth his life" (Proverbs 13:3a).

4. *Those Who Talk Too Much Will Eventually Be Destroyed.* "He that openeth wide his lips shall have destruction" (Proverbs 13:3b).

5. *Right Words Can Turn An Angry Man Into A Friend, And Wrong Words Can Turn A Friend Into An Enemy.* "A soft answer turneth away wrath: but grievous words stir up anger" (Proverbs 15:1).

6. *Your Words Reveal Whether You Are Wise Or A Fool.* "The tongue of the wise useth knowledge aright: but the mouth of fools poureth out foolishness" (Proverbs 15:2).

7. *Right Words Breathe Life Into Everything Around You.* "A wholesome tongue is a tree of life" (Proverbs 15:4a).

8. *The Purpose Of Words Is To Educate, Enthuse, And Enlarge Those Around You.* "The lips of the wise disperse knowledge" (Proverbs 15:7a).

9. *Your Personal Happiness Is Influenced By The Words That Come Out Of Your Own Mouth.* "A man hath joy by the answer of his mouth: and a word spoken in due season, how good is it!" (Proverbs 15:23).

10. *The Wise Are Cautious With Their Words.* "He that hath knowledge spareth his words" (Proverbs 17:27a).

11. *Right Words Are As Important As Water On Earth And The Sustaining Of Human Life.* "The words of a man's mouth are as deep waters, and the wellspring of Wisdom as a flowing brook" (Proverbs 18:4).

12. *Men Fail Because Of The Words They Speak.* "A fools mouth is his destruction, and his lips are the snare of his soul" (Proverbs 18:7).

13. *Wrong Words Wound Others And Destroy*

People And Friendships Forever. "The words of a talebearer are as wounds, and they go down into the innermost parts of the belly" (Proverbs 18:8).

14. *Words Determine Which Dreams Live Or Die.* "Death and life are in the power of the tongue: and they that love it shall eat the fruit thereof" (Proverbs 18:21).

15. *The Words You Allow Others To Speak Into You Is Deciding The Wisdom You Contain.* "Hear counsel, and receive instruction, that thou mayest be wise in thy latter end" (Proverbs 19:20). Solomon knew that words were the difference between his present season and his future season.

16. *Wrong Words Are The Reason Men Fall Into Error.* "Cease, my son, to hear the instruction that causeth to err from the words of knowledge" (Proverbs 19:27).

17. *Good Men Study Their Words Before They Speak Them.* "The heart of the righteous studieth to answer" (Proverbs 15:28a).

18. *The Tongue Is The Major Cause Of All Troubles.* "Whoso keepeth his mouth and his tongue keepeth his soul from troubles" (Proverbs 21:23).

19. *Fools Seldom Understand The Power Of Words.* "Speak not in the ears of a fool: for he will despise the Wisdom of thy words" (Proverbs 23:9).

20. *Talking To Fools Is A Waste Of Time.* "Speak not in the ears of a fool: for he will despise the Wisdom of thy words" (Proverbs 23:9).

21. *Wisdom Is A Result Of The Words You Hear.* "Hear thou, my son, and be wise" (Proverbs 23:19).

22. *The Timing Of Your Words Often Decides*

Your Success Or Failure In A Situation. "A fool uttereth all his mind: but a wise man keepeth it in till afterwards" (Proverbs 29:11).

23. *Influential People Should Use Their Words And Influence To Help The Poor And Needy.* "Open thy mouth, judge righteously, and plead the cause of the poor and needy" (Proverbs 31:9).

24. *The Words Of Wise Women Are Consistently Kind.* "She openeth her mouth with Wisdom; and in her tongue is the law of kindness" (Proverbs 31:26).

25. *Your Words Can Become The Trap That Destroys You.* "Thou art snared with the words of thy mouth" (Proverbs 6:2a).

26. *Right Words Feed And Sustain Those Around You.* "The lips of the righteous feed many: but fools die for want of Wisdom" (Proverbs 10:21).

27. *Right Words Are As Important As Silver And Gold.* "The tongue of the just is as choice silver" (Proverbs 10:20a).

28. *Right Words Can Get You Out Of Any Difficulty And Trouble.* "The mouth of the upright shall deliver them" (Proverbs 12:6b).

29. *Right Words Bring Health And Healing.* "The tongue of the wise is health" (Proverbs 12:18b).

30. *The Wise Avoid The Presence Of Those Who Consistently Speak Wrong Words.* "Go from the presence of a foolish man, when thou perceivest not in him the lips of knowledge" (Proverbs 14:7).

31. *Only The Simple And Fools Believe Everything Others Say.* "The simple believeth every word: but the prudent man looketh well to his going" (Proverbs 14:15).

32. *Right Words Give You Access To Powerful*

And Important People. "Righteous lips are the delight of kings; and they love him that speaketh right" (Proverbs 16:13).

33. *Wisdom Is Necessary In Order To Speak The Right Words.* "The heart of the wise teacheth his mouth, and addeth learning to his lips" (Proverbs 16:23).

34. *Pleasant Words Are The Sweetest Sounds On Earth.* "Pleasant words are as an honeycomb, sweet to the soul, and health to the bones" (Proverbs 16:24).

35. *The Sweetness Of Right Words Could Help To Cure Any Bitterness Existent In The Human Soul.* "Pleasant words are as an honeycomb, sweet to the soul, and health to the bones" (Proverbs 16:24).

36. *The Quality Of Your Words Reveals The Quality Of Your Heart.* "An ungodly man diggeth up evil: and in his lips there is as a burning fire" (Proverbs 16:27). You can read the heart of any person by listening to the words they are speaking about others.

37. *Words Will Quickly Expose Envy And Jealousy Or Admiration And Respect.* "An ungodly man diggeth up evil: and in his lips there is as a burning fire" (Proverbs 16:27).

38. *The Greatest Friendships On Earth Are Broken Because Of Wrong Words.* "A whisperer separateth chief friends" (Proverbs 16:28b).

39. *Strife Can Always Be Traced To Someone's Words.* "A froward man soweth strife" (Proverbs 16:28a).

40. *Evil Is Released Through The Lips.* "Moving his lips he bringeth evil to pass" (Proverbs 16:30b).

41. *You Should Not Answer Anything Until You*

Have Heard All The Details. "He that answereth a matter before he heareth it, it is folly and shame unto him" (Proverbs 18:13). Accuracy is only important when adequate information is available.

42. *Words Influence And Affect The ACCUMU-LATION Of Your Wealth.* "A man's belly shall be satisfied with the fruit of his mouth; and with the increase of his lips shall he be filled" (Proverbs 18:20). This is almost never mentioned in prosperity teaching today. Yet using the wrong words can get you fired or prevent you from getting promoted.

I remember times I was going to give someone a raise until I brought them in and heard the words they were speaking. Complaining, blaming, fault-finding words can stop a boss from promoting you.

44. *Right Words Can Release A Boss To Promote You Or Give You A Raise.* "A man's belly shall be satisfied with the fruit of his mouth; and with the increase of his lips shall he be filled" (Proverbs 18:20).

45. *One Conversation With The Wrong Woman Can Destroy Your Life.* "The mouth of strange women is a deep pit: he that is abhorred of the Lord shall fall therein" (Proverbs 22:14).

46. *Never Enter Into Battle Without Sufficient Counsel.* "For by wise counsel thou shalt make thy war: and in multitude of counsellors there is safety" (Proverbs 24:6).

47. *The Wise Avoid "Self-Praise."* "Let another man praise thee, and not thine own mouth; a stranger, and not thine own lips" (Proverbs 27:2).

48. *Lying Words Can Poison The Attitude Of A Boss Toward An Employee.* "If a ruler hearken to lies, all his servants are wicked" (Proverbs 29:12).

Use every conversation as a practice moment for improving your speech.

That's One of the Secrets of Career Success.

≈ 6 ≈

Take A Small Step Toward Order Every Day.

Success Comes Through Small Steps.

Order and organizing your life is one of these important steps.

Here Are 8 Important Facts About Order And Organizing Your Life

1. *Order Is The Accurate Arrangement Of Things.* Order is placing an item where it belongs. Order is keeping your shirts, ties and shoes in the appropriate place in your closet.

2. *You Were Created For Order.* Anything that slows you down emotionally or mentally will become a distraction.

3. *Order Increases Comfort.* When you walk into a room of order, you want to *stay.* Things are "right." You feel clean, energized and happy. When you walk into a room of clutter and disorder, an unexplainable agitation begins. Perhaps you cannot even name it or understand it.

4. *When You Increase Order In Your Life, You Will Increase Your Productivity.* Filing cabinets, trays

on the desk, and special places for folders make it easier to get your job done *on time*.

5. *Order Eliminates Stress And Agitation.* Have you ever shuffled paper after paper in search of a bill? Of course! When you finally located the bill, you were agitated and angry. It affected your entire day.

Disorder influences your attitude more than you could ever imagine.

6. *Every Tiny Act Of Your Life Will Increase Order Or Disorder Around You.*

7. *Everything You Are Doing Is Affecting Order In Your Life.* Think for a moment. You get up from your breakfast table. Either you will leave your plate on the table, or you will take it to the sink. The decision you make will either increase the order or disorder around you. (Leaving it on the table increases your work load and creates disorder. Taking it to the sink *immediately* brings *order*.)

It happened last night for me. I took off my suit coat and laid it over the chair. I didn't really feel like taking it over to the closet and hanging it up. However, realizing that I was going to have hang it up sooner or later, I walked over to the closet and hung up my coat. *I increased order* around myself immediately.

▶ Every moment you are increasing order or creating disorder around your life.

▶ Small tiny actions can eventually produce chaotic situations.

8. *Every Person Around You Is Increasing Order Or Disorder.* Some people have an *attitude* of disorder. They are unhappy unless everything is in

disarray and cluttered. Others refuse to work in such an environment. Their productivity requires organization.

You Can Get Anywhere You Want to Go If You Are Willing to Take Enough Small Steps.

Somebody has said that the arrangement of things in your garage reveals much about your mind. (Somebody asked me once, "Does this mean if I do not have a garage, that I really do not have a mind either?" (Smile!) I certainly hope that is not the case, but I am certain psychologists have come to some pretty accurate conclusions.)

Why do we permit disorder?

1.   Many of us were raised with those who are unorganized. Large families, busy life-styles, or small, cramped apartments can contribute to our attitude.

2.   Some people do not know how to separate and organize various items around them. They need assistance.

3.   Some people have unusual sensitivity and are simply gifted in keeping order around them.

4.   *Creative people* are often disorganized people. Their focus is change, not permanence. Their attention is on their future, not their present.

5.   *Busy people* moving from place to place are often disorganized. Their mind is on where they are *going* instead of *where they are.*

Some helpful hints:

Recognize the long-term chaos and losses that disorder will create. If this continues, your momentum will eventually destroy you and your productivity. Successes will become fewer.

Take a long, hard and serious look at your personality and what you can do to take steps toward change.

Ask others who are gifted in organization to assist you and keep you on course. (I read where Donald Trump said a that he hired one woman whose entire job is to keep things in order around him.)

Do not berate yourself and become overly critical because of your lack of knowledge, giftings or ability to keep things in order.

Recognize those who God puts close to you who can correct things around you and keep things in order.

Do not try to justify yourself. Relax.

Take a small, tiny step today toward putting things around you in order.

It is commendable that you are planning to take an entire week of your vacation to put everything in order in your house next summer. However, I suggest you begin *this very moment* taking some steps to put things in place here in the room.

Just 20 minutes makes a major difference. Little hinges swing big doors. *You can get anywhere you want to go if you are willing to take enough small steps.*

So, take an important step toward order every moment of your life.

It's One of the Golden Secrets of Career Success.

≈ 7 ≈

NEVER DISCUSS WHAT YOU WANT SOMEONE ELSE TO FORGET.

Your Words Are Pictures. Unforgettable Pictures.
Your words make thoughts become permanent. It's dangerous to speak about things that do not really matter. Your words give life and longevity to everything discussed.

Words keep many things alive. Arguments would die. Conflicts would die. Celebrations would die. Except, your words sustain them.

Words breathe life into everything. "Death and life are in the power of the tongue: and they that love it shall eat the fruit thereof" (Proverbs 18:21).

Words can wound. "The words of a talebearer are as wounds, and they go down into the innermost parts of the belly" (Proverbs 18:8).

"A wholesome tongue is a tree of life" (Proverbs 15:4a).

Even inappropriate words are remembered. Several years ago, a minister had a devastating experience. False accusations were hurled at him. Emotionally shattered, he shared the experience publicly with some of his congregation. Most of them knew nothing about the false accusations *until he brought them out publicly.* It simply created more questions in their minds. Tiny doubts grew like cancer.

"Were they really true after all? Maybe there is another side to the story? Is he telling us everything?"

One by one, he lost supporters. Later, the accusations were proven to be false. But the damage was already done. It was too late.

He had painted scenarios in their minds that time could not erase. His words were photographs that satan could nurture, feed, and grow *in the privacy of their imaginations.*

You cannot stop every one from discussing you. But *never provide them information you want them to forget. Nothing.* Never give unnecessary information that requires or demands or inspires pursuit of more questions.

Be cautious in confessing all your mistakes. Your attempts to "be open" may be very sincere. But your mistake may loom bigger *in their memory* than the lesson you are trying to teach.

People will often remember illustrations for the wrong reasons. Certainly, there are unusual moments when additional information and clarification is advisable, beneficial and even necessary. But this is rare.

Focus on your future, not yesterday.

Never say anything you do not want to hear about for the rest of your life.

That's One of the Secrets of Career Success.

≈ 8 ≈

RECOGNIZE AND FOLLOW THE PATH OF FAVOR.

Favor Is Not Merely An Experience.

Favor is the divine current that takes you from your present season into your future dream.

Favor is the Golden River from your pit to your palace. It is not a mere experience of someone doing nice things for you.

Here Are 20 Facts You Should Know About Favor

1. *Favor Is When Someone Has A Desire To Solve A Problem For You.* Your own attitude determines God's attitude toward you. Follow the path of favor *wherever it is happening* in your life today. Who has discerned your worth? Who feels *kindly* toward your life? Who has been *the source most used by God* in your financial life within the last 12 months? Who has been your greatest source of spiritual *encouragement* and maturity? Who does God seem to be using *right now to open appropriate doors* for your life? Who is the Golden Connection that could easily shorten the trip that you've been taking toward your dream?

Recognize the *path*.

Recognize the *person*.

God is presently using them for this *season*. (Stop evaluating their flaws. Stop building walls of distrust. Is God using them in your own life *right now*?)

2. *Favor Is Not An Accident*. God uses favor as a reward for even small acts of obedience to His principles. "If ye be willing and obedient, ye shall eat the good of the land;" (Isaiah 1:19).

3. *Favor Is Not A Normality*. Millions struggle and sweat every day of their lives to advance a single inch. They have not tasted the flow of uncommon favor. "Except the Lord build the house, they labour in vain that build it:" (Psalm 127:1).

4. *Favor Is Not A Guarantee*. You see, everyone does *not* qualify. You must do certain things to qualify for uncommon favor. "And it shall come to pass, if thou shalt hearken diligently unto the voice of the Lord thy God, to observe and to do all His commandments which I command thee this day, that the Lord thy God will set thee on high above all nations of the earth: And all these blessings shall come on thee, and overtake thee, if thou shalt hearken unto the voice of the Lord thy God" (Deuteronomy 28:1,2).

5. *Favor Is A Gift From God*. He does not owe it to you. You cannot purchase it. Others are not obligated to you. (When you obligate others, you create a potential enemy. Those acts are called favors, not favor.) "He that openeth, and no man shutteth," (Revelation 3:7).

6. *Favor Is Necessary For Uncommon Success*. You cannot work hard enough to get everything you

deserve and want. You cannot work enough jobs to generate the finances you will need for all your dreams and goals. Others owe you nothing. Yet favor is *necessary* for you to take giant leaps into your future. "The Lord thy God shall bless thee in all thine increase, and in all the works of thine hands," (Deuteronomy 16:15).

7. *Favor Begins When You Solve A Problem For Someone.* When Joseph interpreted the dream for Pharaoh, his gift made room for him. He was promoted to the second place of power, Prime Minister. "And Pharaoh took off his ring from his hand, and put it upon Joseph's hand, and arrayed him in vestures of fine linen, and put a gold chain about his neck; And he made him to ride in the second chariot which he had; and they cried before him, Bow the knee: and he made him ruler over all the land of Egypt. And Pharaoh said unto Joseph, I am Pharaoh, and without thee shall no man lift up his hand or foot in all the land of Egypt" (Genesis 41:42-44).

8. *Favor Can Accelerate Your Destiny.* It shortens the distance of your journey. Jonah was three days from Nineveh. But after his repentance, he arrived in one day. He shortened his trip through repentance and humility. After two years, Joseph was still in prison because of false accusations. Within 24 hours, he became Prime Minister. That is *acceleration* of your destiny. When the currents of favor flow, you can achieve in a day what has taken you 20 years in the past.

9. *Favor Is Not Stagnant.* It is a current that increases from a trickle to a Niagara Falls, when it

is honored and embraced. Few respect it long enough to taste its momentum and full harvest. "But other fell into good ground, and brought forth fruit, some an hundredfold," (Matthew 13:8).

10. *Favor Can Grow.* Jesus grew in favor with God and man (see Luke 2:52). The good happening for you today can increase one hundred times within the next 12 months. "Then Peter began to say unto Him, Lo, we have left all, and have followed Thee. And Jesus answered and said, Verily I say unto you, There is no man that hath left house, or brethren, or sisters, or father, or mother, or wife, or children, or lands, for My sake, and the gospel's, But he shall receive an hundredfold now in this time, houses, and brethren, and sisters, and mothers, and children, and lands, with persecutions; and in the world to come eternal life" (Mark 10:28-30).

11. *Favor Is A Seed You Can Sow Into Others. Everyone has the ability to Sow favor.* Solving problems are Seeds of favor. Enabling others to succeed reveals favor. When you help others achieve their goals, you are sowing favor. "Knowing that whatsoever good thing any man doeth, the same shall he receive of the Lord, whether he be bond or free" (Ephesians 6:8).

12. *Favor Begins As A Seed And Ends As A Harvest.* What you sow today will reenter your life in your future. This is the Harvest of Favor. "Be not deceived; God is not mocked: for whatsoever a man soweth, that shall he also reap" (Galatians 6:7).

13. *Favor Comes When Others Pray For You.* Peter was imprisoned. But the church prayed, and God became involved. The doors of the prison were

opened. Peter was released (see Acts 12:5).

14. *Favor Can Stop A Tragedy Instantly.* Favor prevents tragedies. It moved Joseph from the prison to the palace in 24 hours. "And Pharaoh said unto Joseph...Thou shalt be over my house, and according unto thy word shall all my people be ruled..." (Genesis 41:39-40). When Jonah cried out on the streets of Nineveh, favor flowed. God had sent Jonah to warn the Ninevites. When the king called a fast, the favor of God was birthed (see Jonah 3:10).

15. *Favor Can Make You Wealthy In One Day.* The peasant Ruth became the wife of wealthy Boaz. "So Boaz took Ruth, and she was his wife:" (Ruth 4:13).

16. *Favor Can Make You A Household Name In 24 Hours.* Favor put a young Jewish lady into the position of queen within a day. "So Esther was taken unto king Ahasuerus into his house royal in the tenth month," (Esther 2:16).

17. *Favor Can Double Your Financial Worth.* It doubled Job's blessing at the end of his trial. "And the Lord turned the captivity of Job, when he prayed for his friends: also the Lord gave Job twice as much as he had before. Then came there unto him all his brethren, and all his sisters, and all they that had been of his acquaintance before, and did eat bread with him in his house: and they bemoaned him, and comforted him over all the evil that the Lord had brought upon him: every man also gave him a piece of money, and every one an earring of gold. So the Lord blessed the latter end of Job more than his beginning:" (Job 42:10-12).

18. *Favor Can Stop When You Deliberately*

Ignore An Instruction From God. Saul ignored the instructions of Samuel to kill King Agag, and all the Amalekites. Favor stopped. God altered the monarchy and David became king. "But Saul and the people spared Agag...Then came the word of the Lord unto Samuel, saying, It repenteth me that I have set up Saul to be king...for thou hast rejected the word of the Lord, and the Lord hath rejected thee from being king over Israel" (1 Samuel 15:9-11, 26).

Nebuchadnezzar experienced uncommon success. When he became filled with pride, God let him become like a beast in the field for seven years. "But when his heart was lifted up, and his mind hardened in pride, he was deposed from his kingly throne, and they took his glory from him...and his heart was made like the beasts," (Daniel 5:20-21).

19. *Favor Stops When The Tithe Is Withheld From God.* A curse comes instead of a blessing. "Will a man rob God? Yet ye have robbed Me. But ye say, Wherein have we robbed Thee? In tithes and offerings. Ye are cursed with a curse: for ye have robbed Me, even this whole nation" (Malachi 3:8-9).

20. *Few Are Truly Knowledgeable Of The Power And Principles Of Favor.* It is rarely studied. Rarely protected. It is considered an accident, a guarantee or a normality. But it is none of these. "My people are destroyed for lack of knowledge:" (Hosea 4:6).

Follow where your currents of favor are taking you.

That's One of the Golden Secrets of Career Success.

❧ 9 ❧

Re-Assess And Evaluate Your Personal Goals Continually.

———◦———

Your Goals Will Change Throughout Your Life.
Someday, you will look back at this very moment and be amazed at the goals you presently have. Things so vital to you at 20 years of age will become unimportant to you at 30.

When I was beginning my ministry, I wanted very much to minister in many different states and cities. Times have changed. Needs have changed. My personal goals have changed. Today, staying home excites me. Knowing that my books are being read in many places is far more satisfying to me than traveling. The greatest goal of my life today is staying in my Secret Place of prayer and writing what the Holy Spirit teaches me through His Word and daily experiences.

These kinds of good changes will happen to you, too.

Here Are 6 Helpful Tips Concerning Your Dreams And Goals

1. *Invest One Hour In Writing Down Clearly The Goals That Really Matter To You At This Point.*

You keep it confidential and private. "Write the vision, and make it plain upon tables, that he may run that readeth it" (Habakkuk 2:2).

2. *Permit Unexciting Dreams Of Yesterday To die.* Stop pursuing something that does not have the ability to excite you any more. Don't feel obligated to keep trying to obtain it...if you are in a different place in your life (see Isaiah 43:18,19).

3. *Do Not Depend On Others To Understand Your Dreams And Goals.* Permit them their individuality, also. They have every right to love the things they love. But refuse to be intimidated by their efforts to persuade you to move in a different direction with your life.

4. *Never Make Permanent Decisions Because Of Temporary Feelings.* (One young lady got so excited about a new friend, she dropped the lease on her own apartment and moved into the apartment of her friend. Within a week, she realized her mistake!)

5. *Avoid Intimate Relationships With Those Who Do Not Really Respect Your Dreams.* You will have to sever ties. *Wrong people do not always leave your life voluntarily.* Life is too short to permit discouragers close to you. "And have no fellowship with the unfruitful works of darkness, but rather reprove them" (Ephesians 5:11).

6. *Anticipate Changes In Your Goals.* Your present feelings and opinions are not permanent. New experiences are coming. New relationships are ahead. Stay conscious of this.

When you assess and evaluate your goals, you will unclutter your life of the unnecessary.

That's One of the Secrets of Career Success.

≈ 10 ≈

Listen To One Mentorship Tape Daily.

Your Daily Habits Produce Powerful Results.
Last night, I flew in from a crusade in Houston. I arrived at 9:30 p.m., but had to remain on the runway for a long time due to early arrival. It was midnight when I finally arrived home. Though tired, I ran my bath water and relaxed. The day had been a full one. I did not feel like reading, cleaning up my house or anything else. But I knew the power of simply *listening*. So I played a cassette tape by one of the most effective business writers in America. He was interviewing a major motivation speaker. It was tremendous, stimulating, and gave me answers.

Though I was too fatigued to study, my time for bathing and getting ready for bed was not wasted either. The tape was still playing when I drifted off to sleep an hour later.

Here Are 8 Tips In Receiving Daily Mentoring Through Tapes

1. *Respect Mentors.* Mentors are those who know something you do not know, have been where you want to go and have done something significant that you would like to accomplish.

Do not lose precious moments with them.

2.   *Recognize That Mentorship Can Take Place Any Moment Of The Day.* Plan *ahead* for such moments. While getting dressed, cleaning up your room or eating lunch alone, you can listen to tapes.

3.   *Listen To The Same Tape Repeatedly.* You will often miss important information the first time. Listen *again.* When you hear something vital, stop the tape and *play it back.*

4.   *Keep Notes On Each Tape.* Write down memorable keys in a special notebook. (I call mine, "The Wisdom Encyclopedia.")

5.   *Picture The Truths As You Listen.* Visualization is a powerful way to *keep something that you're hearing.*

6.   *Talk To Others Daily About The Secrets You Are Learning.*

7.   *Keep The Mentorship Tapes In Front Of You On A Shelf.* Take advantage of each spare moment and have them accessible.

8.   *Listen To A Variety Of Speakers.* Do not limit yourself to one school of thought. Listen to businessmen, motivation speakers, missionaries, pastors, and evangelists. Every person has been given a different view and experienced a variety of events in their lives. *Learn from many.* The Holy Spirit used 40 different authors over a 1600 year period to document the Scriptures. Each author was inspired to focus on something different...*for a reason.*

Listen daily to Wisdom tapes. It could stop a thousand heartaches and birth your greatest dream.

It's One of the Secrets of Career Success.

≈ 11 ≈

ALWAYS PAY YOUR VOWS.

Vows Are Not Frivolous Things To God.
Vows to God.
Vows to family.
Vows to your boss.
Vows to employees.
Vows to yourself.
God is not playful, frivolous or trivial.

God takes your promises to Him quite seriously.
"Better is it that thou shouldest not vow, than thou should vow and not pay" (Ecclesiastes 5:5).

God calls promise breakers, fools. "When thou vowest a vow unto God, defer not to pay it; for He hath no pleasure in fools: pay that which thou hast vowed" (Ecclesiastes 5:4). That's why it is so important not to position yourself as a fool. Fools are ultimately destroyed. He *humiliates* fools. He moves *away* from fools. He uses fools as illustrations for *destruction*.

God wants you to keep your promises. To your family. To your spouse. To the Lord Who promised you His best. It is important that you develop impeccable and unwavering integrity when you give your word in a business transaction or to your children.

God is a covenant God. He sees the vows you have made before Him and men.

Oh, stop and reexamine your life this very moment. Have you made any financial vows to your church or the man of God in your life? Pay them.

Whatever it takes, pay your vows.

Paying your vows can break "the curse." When you keep your vow, God's very best begins to come to you. Read Deuteronomy 28 and Leviticus 26 to see the incredible blessings that come to those who "observe and to do all his commandments" (Deuteronomy 28:1).

After an anointed banquet one evening, an articulate and well-dressed lady approached me.

"I know God has spoken to me tonight to plant a $1,000 Seed into your ministry. You will receive it in a few days," she said wiping tears of joy from her eyes.

A few days later, her letter arrived. It was an apology. "After I talked to my husband, I felt that I should break my promise to you. I do not believe we can really afford to sow this special Seed at this time," she wrote.

Tragic. You see, while she was in the presence of God and the anointing of the Holy Spirit was hovering over the congregation, the Seeds of her faith exploded within her heart. God spoke. She heard. She moved swiftly to declare her covenant with God. After she moved *away* from His presence and discussed this gigantic step of faith with an unbelieving husband, *she withdrew from the covenant* which she had entered into with God. Only time will reveal the curse such an attitude of frivolity and light-heartedness will produce in our lives!

God convicted me of a forgotten vow. I was

sitting in my bed watching a religious television program. Suddenly, a famous evangelist looked into the camera and said so forcibly, "If you have made a vow to God at any time and not paid it, you have launched a parade of tragedies. Please sit down today and *pay your vows.*"

Conviction smote my heart.

Over two years before, I had promised a missionary in Africa that I would help sponsor some students for scholarships in his Bible college. I had asked him to rush me information about it. When I did not receive the information, I did nothing. I did not telephone him or pursue a reason. I simply used it as an excuse to "escape my vow" that I had made to him.

As I felt my heart pound, I asked God to "Please forgive me. Give me another chance. Do not withhold your harvest from me." It was midnight, but I called my secretary anyway. "Whatever you do, when you arrive at the office tomorrow morning, please take the checkbook and write out a check to this Bible school in East Africa. Airmail it. I cannot live another day without the blessing of God flowing upon me. I cannot afford a curse on my life and ministry," I explained to her.

Countless thousands lift their hands and make faith promises, "Yes, I will plant a special Seed *each month* to help you spread the Wisdom of God." Yet, over 50 percent will never sit down and plant that Seed that they vowed publicly to plant.

"Maybe they cannot afford to do it!" is a common explanation.

I have seen many people make this claim, yet

they continue to get salary raises, new television sets, new clothes and send their children through college. Throughout all of this spending, they make the same claim: "I really cannot keep my faith promise."

"Would you like for me to ask God to make you as poor as you tell everybody you really are?" asked the minister of a disgruntled parishioner one Sunday morning.

When you make a faith promise, it is a covenant between you and God. Do not treat it lightly. Make every effort to pay it.

If you do not have enough finances to pay your vow at one time, plant *small Seeds as often as possible* and your own harvest will increase. Then you will find it possible to complete your faith promise and vow, as He blesses you.

If you truly feel that you have made a hasty decision, then ask the Lord to give you *an extra miracle* so that you can complete your faith vow to Him in a *supernatural way.*

The man of God is not really authorized to "let you off." This faith promise is between *you and God*, and must be settled between you both.

Unpaid vows are a powerful reason thousands have never tasted the reward of their step of faith.

Pay your vows and *favor will flow.*

It's One of the Secrets of Career Success.

≫ 12 ≫

Use Equipment Or Machines To Do A Job Whenever Possible.

Proper Equipment Increases Your Productivity.
Never have someone do a job that a machine can do instead. This is a humorous explanation of the advantages of proper machines.

10 Advantages In Using Appropriate Technology

1.   Machines Do Not *Require Coaxing*, Just Repair.

2.   Machines Do Not Get *Discouraged* When Their Mother-in-law Comes To Town.

3.   Machines Are Never *Disloyal*, Discussing Your Secrets With Everyone Else.

4.   Your Machines Will Not *File Grievance Reports* Against You When You Fail To Meet Their Expectations.

5.   Machines Do Not Require *Medical Insurance*, Sick Leave Or Time Off.

6.   Machines Can Be *Replaced* Quickly And Easily Without Breaking Your Heart.

7.   Machines Do Not *Request A Retirement Fund* And Want To Be Paid For The Years Ahead When They Do Not Perform.

8. Machines Never Come To Work *Late* And Want To *Leave Early*.

9. Machines Will Work *Through* Lunch, Requiring No "Break Time."

10. Machines Never Interrupt The Productivity Of *Other Machines,* Slowing Down The Entire Project.

6 Qualities Of An Uncommon Employee. They will:

1. *Find The Most Effective Equipment Possible To Do Their Present Job.*

2. *Telephone Other Businesses Or Companies To Locate Appropriate Or Needed Machines And Equipment.*

3. *Attend Seminars And Workshops That Increase Their Efficiency Or Skills On Computers And Other Machines.*

4. *Inform Their Boss What Is Needed To Do The Job More Efficiently,* more accurately and quickly. (He will usually do anything possible to make the hours of employees more effective and productive.)

5. *Continuously Evaluate Their Work.* What is slowing them down? What machine could make a big difference in the completion of their daily tasks and responsibilities?

6. *Present Their Supervisors With Options, Costs And Potential Benefits Of Purchasing More Machines.* Your staff will treasure it and learn to appreciate their own work load reduction because of it. It decreases the opportunities for mistakes. It increases their sense of progress and accomplishment.

Search for appropriate equipment to accomplish your tasks quickly.

That's One of the Secrets of Career Success.

≈ 13 ≈

Learn From The Best, Not Only The Accessible.

———————

Advisors Are Everywhere.
But, you need to pursue the qualified, not the available. "A wise man will hear, and will increase learning; and a man of understanding shall attain unto wise counsels:" (Proverbs 1:5).

Recently, a young pastor was discussing his difficulties with me.   His ministry seemed to be a collection of tragedies and disappointments.

"Who is your mentor?" I suddenly asked.

He stumbled around a bit. He seemed uneasy and uncomfortable. So I persisted.

"Well, there is a preacher that I talk to occasionally in the next town," he answered.

"Is he truly effective?" I asked.

"No, not really. But, he is someone to talk to," was his defensive reply.

I insisted that he needed a worthy *mentor.* A *capable* mentor. Someone who knew what they were talking about.

"Would *you* consider becoming my mentor?" he asked.

"I am not even a pastor! Besides I am too busy

with my own Assignment of writing, speaking and traveling. But you need to learn from someone who is the *best* at what they do—*pastoring*."

I connected him to two friends of mine who are very effective pastors. You see, it is not enough to receive advice. It is not enough to have a mentor.

You can only learn the best from The Best.

When you want to improve your game of Ping-Pong, you must play someone who is *better* than you.

When you want to increase, you must sit at the feet of someone who *knows more* than you.

Learning from The Best may be *intimidating*. They will demand more from you than anyone else.

It is usually *uncomfortable*.

But it guarantees increase.

It is the Road to Greatness.

Most simply want someone who is accessible and *within reach*. But it is more important to *pursue the qualified, not merely the available*. When I hire an attorney, I do not want someone who is merely inexpensive or near my home. I want someone who truly cares, has proven themselves in court and is known for their thoroughness of preparation.

Some attend a church because it's near their house. How ridiculous! That's like marrying a man because he lives closer to your house than other men.

Learning from The Best will take the investment of time. Search for those who have established their reputations and standards as *the highest*.

If you want to help a small church, find out *who* is mentoring the young pastor of that church. When he sits at someone's feet who is skilled, *you* will receive the benefits. If he is unteachable, you will taste the bitterness of every mistake and wrong decision he makes. There are hair salons close to my house. But I drive further to the young man who is the best. He does it right. He listens to me. He is not merely accessible.

Those who pursue convenience will never taste the heights of excellence. If you are willing to inconvenience yourself in the pursuit of excellence, you will create the most remarkable and uncommon life you have ever imagined.

Do not purchase clothes simply because they are "on sale." Purchase clothes that present you *properly*, make you *feel* wonderful, and make you want to wear them *every day* of your life. I never purchase anything that I will wear only once. I want the best out of everything that I invest in.

Learning from The Best may require your willingness to live on a lower income right now.

A pastor picked me up from the airport recently. He told me something interesting about his son. His son had accepted a job at a much lower salary with another pastor. The reason? That specific pastor, though he paid a lower salary, was a superb *mentor*. His own success was remarkable. The young man had enough sense to accept a job with lower salary...*so that he could learn from the very best.*

Learning from The Best may necessitate a geographical change. You might have to move from where you are to another state. *Do it, if that is what it takes.*

Remember the true reason you are there.

Remember the specific knowledge you are trying

to learn. If you are sitting at the feet of a great electrician, he may know little about protocol. But, you are not there to learn about protocol. You are there to learn about electricity.

You will not learn everything from one person during your life. Do not attempt it. It is too much stress on them. You will be disappointed. God never intended for you to do so. *Many* are necessary to make you successful, learned and skilled throughout your life.

Always sit at the feet of The Best.

It's One of the Secrets of Career Success.

❧ 14 ❧

Become Knowledgeable Of The Most Important Success Book In The World.

The Holy Bible Is Your Success Handbook.

It occurred to me this morning, while my father and I were in prayer, what I would not know had the Bible never been given to me. Take a moment and think about it's benefits for *you.*

10 Rewards In Knowing The Word Of God

1. *You Discover The Weapons God Gas Given You For All Of Your Battles With Satan And Evil Spirits.* Praise is a weapon. His words are weapons. Resisting satan can create his departure (see Ephesians 6:11-17).

2. *Your Enemy Has Fears.* Satan fears your knowledge of the Word of God (see Matthew 4 and Luke 4).

3. *Angels Are Assigned To Help You* (see Hebrews 1:13-14). Invisible companies surround you daily to protect you and minister to you.

4. *The Holy Spirit Is Within You And Beside You.* His power and presence are *accessed through singing* (see Psalm 100:2).

5. *You Know How To Judge The Behavior, The Conduct, And The Words Of Other Men.* You would be deceived a thousand times more if you didn't have the standard of the Scriptures to judge others.

6. *Your Life Of Integrity Is Promised A Reward System In The Scriptures.* The Holy Spirit promises rewards for your obedience, for the battles that you win, for each labor of love that He mentions in Scripture (see Matthew 10:42 and also Mark 9:41).

7. *Heaven Is An Ultimate Reward For You If You Endure And Live A Life A Holy Life.* "In my Father's house are many mansions..." (John 14:2).

8. *Hell Is The Torment Of Eternity Produced If You Do Not Live For God.* "And he cried and said, Father Abraham, have mercy on me, and send Lazarus, that he may dip the tip of his finger in water, and cool my tongue; for I am tormented in this flame," (Luke 16:24).

9. *You Would Have No Motivation In Yourself To Withdraw From Evil And Abandon Yourself To Righteousness.* The Word of God keeps convicting you.

10. *No Parent Would Have Any Authoritative Guidelines For Child Rearing.* "Wherewithal shall a young man cleanse his way? by taking heed thereto according to Thy word," (Psalm 119:9).

Embrace the Holy Word of God with all your heart. *Everything* you need to know to *succeed* in your life—is in the Word of God.

It's One of the Secrets of Career Success.

≈ 15 ≈

Keep One Master Address Book.

Friendship Deserves Care And Attention.
Successful people treasure worthy friendships.
Names are vital. Building a significant rolodex or
address book is a *must*. Keep in touch regularly with
those who love you.

*Every successful pastor knows the importance
of a name.* That's why visitor cards are given out at
most services. Receptions where greeters meet
newcomers are held every Sunday morning. Millions
of dollars are spent on television programs, radio
broadcasts and newspaper ads—because of the
names of those who are important to their vision.

*Every successful businessman knows the
importance of a single name.* Listen to Ron Popeil, a
multimillionaire who has enjoyed great success.
"One of the mandates at Ronco, besides quality and
innovation, is this: A name, address, and phone
number are worth gold. We always capture a
telephone number in addition to the name and
address of a customer, because those items are very
common, very valuable." (Page 219, *The Salesman
of the Century.*)

*Avoid keeping names and addresses in many
different places.*

Keep one Master Address Book.

I call mine, "The Problem Solvers."

My dentist's name is kept under "D." When I want to buy carpet, I look under "C" where I have placed the business card of a local carpet store.

Think of everyone around you as a potential problem solver for your life. Treasure your access to them. When you receive a business card, place it under the divider most appropriate. For instance, if you meet Mr. Sam Jones who sells automobiles, don't put his business card under "J" for Jones. You won't remember it a year later. Place his business card under "A" for automobiles.

Friendships are too precious to lose. They cost too much to treat lightly. I once read where one of our U.S. Presidents had 7,500 names in his rolodex. He loved people. He valued people. He knew the importance of a name.

Build a Master Address Book of those who truly matter to your life.

It's One of the Secrets of Career Success.

❧ 16 ❧

WALK AWAY FROM UNNECESSARY CONFLICT.

━━━━►❁◄━━━━

Most Battles Are Not Really Important.

Here Are 16 Important Facts About Conflicts And Contentious People

1. *Conflict Distracts You From Your Dreams And Goals.* By the way, a contentious person often considers himself very honest and up front. In fact, they usually take pride in telling you "the way things really are." Subconsciously, they are often modeling someone in their life (a father or mother) who accomplished their goals through *intimidation*. Subconsciously, they admire this person and have decided to follow that pattern, failing to see the *losses* created through this kind of attitude.

2. *Nothing Is More Harmful To A Company Than A Contentious Employee.* Every boss knows this. When an employee cannot get along with other employees, profits are lost. That employee becomes costly. Focus is broken. Other employees become emotionally fragmented. Important projects are delayed.

3. *Contentious People Destroy The Momentum, Bonding And Synergy That Agreement Can Create.*

"Mark them which cause divisions and offenses...avoid them" (Romans 16:17).

"And the servant of the Lord must not strive; but be gentle unto all men, apt to teach, patient," (2 Timothy 2:24).

4.   *Contentious People Are In Total Opposition To The Law Of Agreement, The Greatest Law Of Success On Earth.* "Two are better than one; because they have a good reward for their labour. For if they fall, the one will lift up his fellow: but woe to him that is alone when he falleth; for he hath not another to help him up" (Ecclesiastes 4:9,10).

5.   *The Character Of A Contentious Person Is Only Revealed When You Rebuke Them.* If he is a scorner and fool, he will hate you. If he is a wise person simply needing correction, he will love you. "Reprove not a scorner, lest he hate thee: rebuke a wise man, and he will love thee" (Proverbs 9:8).

6.   *Contentious People Discuss Situations That Do Not Involve Them.* This is one of the evidences of a contentious person. They discuss the business of *others*. "He that passeth by, and meddleth with strife belonging not to him, is like one that taketh a dog by the ears" (Proverbs 26:17).

7.   *A Contentious Person Enjoys Debate, Disputings And Opposing Whatever Has Been Spoken.* A contentious person always looks for a reason to disagree about something. They *ignore* every point of *agreement*.

8.   *A Contentious Person Is Always A Door For Satan To Launch Every Evil Work In An Organization.* "For where envying and strife is, there is confusion and every evil work" (James 3:16).

9.   *A Contentious Person Is In Opposition To*

Godly Wisdom. "But the Wisdom that is from above is first pure, then peaceable, gentle, and easy to be intreated, full of mercy and good fruits, without partiality, and without hypocrisy" (James 3:17).

10. *A Contentious Attitude And Spirit Is Always Birthed By Unthankfulness.* It is a sin that God abhors. It was the first sin ever committed. Satan was unthankful for his position and chose to fight for a change. *Ingratitude is poisonous.* It can destroy a family within weeks. It can ruin a successful organization within months. Churches exploding with growth have fragmented within weeks when a spirit of ingratitude infected the congregation.

11. *Any Contentious Conversation Must Be Boldly Faced And Stopped Immediately.* Interrupt the conversation with, "It's wonderful how God will *turn this* for our good! I am so thankful for what He is about to do! Don't we have a wonderful God!" It will be like throwing cold water on a destructive fire.

12. *The Contentious Person Must Be Confronted Honestly And Courageously About Their Attitude.* Others are bold enough to poison your climate and atmosphere with Arrows of Unthankfulness piercing the air. So, dominate your turf. Take charge. Use *your* words to turn the tide.

13. *Contentious People Often Sabotage The Work Of God.* Many years ago I heard one of the most startling statements from a famous missionary. I was sitting under some huge trees in East Africa. Monkeys were jumping from tree limb to tree limb. My precious missionary friend explained the number one reason some missionaries never fulfill their full term on the field. (I thought missionaries came home

due to sickness, culture shock or lack of finances.)

"Mike, the number one reason missionaries do not stay on the mission field is their *inability to get along with the other missionaries.*" Think about it. Missionaries who should be obsessed with sharing the Gospel, often return home because of the failure to create harmony and an environment of agreement.

14. *Contention Is Contagious.* When someone permits the spirit of conflict and disputing to enter their life, they will influence and affect *everyone around them.* I have seen a happy, peaceful household dissolve into arguments within 30 minutes of the arrival of a contentious person. That person *carried* the spirit of contention with them.

15. *Any Contentious Person Who Refuses To Change Must Not Continue To Have Access To You.* "Where no wood is, there the fire goeth out: so where there is no talebearer, the strife ceaseth. As coals are to burning coals, and wood to fire; so is a contentious man to kindle strife" (Proverbs 26:20,21). *Your attitude is a personal decision.* Your attitude is a mood created by your chosen focus.

16. *You Can Succeed Almost Anywhere Else, Except With A Contentious Person.* "It is better to dwell in the corner of the housetop, than with a brawling woman and in a wide house" (Proverbs 25:24).

Remember, conflict always begins with a person, not merely an issue, "Where no wood is, there the fire goeth out: so where there is no talebearer, the strife ceaseth" (Proverbs 26:20). Agreement is the greatest enemy Satan has ever faced. Walk away from contentious people.

This is One of the Secrets of Career Success.

～ 17 ～

STOP RUSHING
THROUGH LIFE.

Your Day Should Be Savored, Not Gulped Down.
Your life is a glorious gift from your Creator.
Do not rush through it. Look at each day like a
wonderful fountain. Take a deep drink from the
sweet waters of the *Present*. You see, Today is really
the only place you will ever exist. When you get to
your future, you will rename it—*Today.*

Yesterday is in the *tomb.*

Tomorrow is in the *womb.*

Your life is *Today.*

If you do not know how to enjoy today, you
probably will not enjoy many days in your future.

Happiness is a now place. It is not a future
destination. "This is the day which the Lord hath
made; we will rejoice and be glad in it" (Psalm
118:24).

*Savor this moment because the future is not
guaranteed.* "Whereas ye know not what shall be on
the morrow. For what is your life? It is even a vapour,
that appeareth for a little time, and then vanisheth
away" (James 4:14).

Surrender totally to Jesus today. (Tomorrow
may be too late.) "Behold, now is the accepted time;
behold, now is the day of salvation," (2 Corinthians
6:2b).

Do not over-schedule yourself today. Some tasks require *quality* time. You can do them with greater excellence tomorrow.

Raise your present turf to its highest level of excellence today. Do it with all your might.

Insist that every moment be a moment of excellence. Whatever you do, do it with all your heart. *Converse* at the highest level. *Exercise* accurately. *Plan* thoroughly, but not hurriedly.

Hurried lives are not necessarily productive lives. Busyness is not always a forward and progressive movement. I've been around people who "flurry." Their emotional energy is higher than anyone around them, yet, nothing significant occurs.

Calm and gentle people are not necessarily slow in their productivity. Some of the most extraordinary achievers are methodical, unhurried and thoughtful. Their *decisions* are significant. Their instructions are *clear* and defined. Precision marks *every* step. Progress is the proof of effectiveness, not mere energy.

My own life is quite scheduled. Yesterday, I finished a conference in Virginia and took a plane to Pittsburgh. Then, I changed planes to fly to Ohio. I dictated two chapters in a new book, reviewed 20 to 30 pages of faxes, wrote letters, and telephoned seven pastors and friends. Then, I spoke at a special banquet for a church where $200,000 was committed to a new house of the Lord. The pastor met me this morning, drove me to the airport where I continued to dictate en route. I *read* on the plane, *dozed* a bit, and came straight to the hotel upon arrival. Now, I'm in Florida.

Yet, nothing is in a frenzy around me.

Let me explain. When I walked into my

beautiful suite here in Tampa, I took my cassette recorder out of my briefcase. Praise music filled this beautiful hotel room. I began to praise and worship and thank God for the wonderful life He has given me. The service will begin in three hours. While waiting for room service to arrive, I went downstairs to receive a new book mailed from my printer. I unpacked my luggage and within moments my meal arrived. The atmosphere in this hotel room is marvelous. The Holy Spirit is here in an incredible way. I am not alone. *He is here*—my *focus,* my *life* and my *joy.* Millions attempt to fill their lives with activities, new friends and "things." *I refuse to race through life.*

I will *walk* through the Garden of Life.

I will smell the roses of His presence, drinking deep from the Fountain of Peace. Sometimes deadlines may require me to *double up* to complete a major goal, but I will walk, *not race* through life.

9 Ways To Getting The Most Out Of Your Day

1. *Write Out A Basic Plan For Each Day.* Link each task to the *time* you want to do it. Evaluate and prioritize each task. Always work on tasks in the order of their reward and benefits back to you.

2. *Concentrate On The Tasks That Really Produce Quality Results.* Moving decisively with purpose is the opposite of lethargy and indifference. When you see someone move deliberately, it may not necessarily be due to a lack of energy, or caring. It is often the opposite. It is totally focusing on doing the job with excellence.

3. *Always Give Total Attention To The Task At Hand.* As the Apostle Paul said, "Brethren, I count not myself to have apprehended: but this one thing I do, forgetting those things which are behind, and reaching forth unto those things which are before," (Philippians 3:13).

4. *Drink Deeply From The Present Moment.* Remember, it took you a long time to get here. *Savor it.*

5. *Stay Sensitive To The Schedules Of Others.* When their own duties become burdensome, accommodate them. Either assist them or move out of their way!

6. *Slow Down Your Eating. Eat slowly* tasting the wonderful provision of God. Don't hurry your eating. Doctors tell us that this is the *best* way to eat. This had been a challenge for me, personally. I am normally a very fast eater. Eating has always been an interruption, not an event. However, as the Holy Spirit has been helping me, I have been making meal time a wonderful time of meditation, review and *thankfulness.*

7. *Look For Qualities You Love* In Others And *Express* Your Gratitude. Avoid agitation.

8. *Look For Things To Enjoy*, Not Endure. What you look for, you will eventually see.

9. *Talk Continually To The Holy Spirit About Every Decision You Are Making. Ask* for uncommon Wisdom, Favor and Strength. "And whatsoever ye shall ask in My name, that will I do, that the Father may be glorified in the Son," (John 14:13).

Stop hurrying through the Garden of Life.

It's One of the Secrets of Career Success.

≈ 18 ≈

Remind Yourself Continuously That There Is Something In Those Around You That You Have Not Yet Discerned.

We Rarely Discern Others Accurately.

Almost every conclusion we have about others is flawed, inadequate and insufficient. We quit on others, because we cannot see *what God is seeing.* God hasn't quit. He placed something *inside* them that we cannot see.

Those closest to you have an incredible future. It might intimidate you if you knew how great it really is. In fact, you would probably be investing more time and energy in knowing them if you really could see what God is planning to do through their lives!

God is looking at something He placed within them *that you cannot yet see. Withhold your words of judgment.* God is not finished growing them. *Withhold words of criticism.*

God saw qualities in David that his own brothers could not see. Yet, he appears cocky and proud. But within hours after he kills Goliath his name will be a household word in Israel. Get along with him. God might use him as a key to your own future.

Look twice at your brothers and sisters again. (Think of Joseph!) The brother who agitates you might become Prime Minister. So, create memories that will foster *respect*.

Look past outward appearances. The thin wall of clothing is so deceptive. Remember Ruth? She's a peasant bowed low, gathering barley. Her stringy hair and tattered clothes *conceal* her *future*. She will become the future wife of your boss, Boaz! She will someday sign your paycheck. So, leave those *handfuls of purpose to bless her* (Ruth 2:16).

Look beyond the distraction of beauty. Remember the beautiful Queen Esther? Consider the fool, Haman. He has misjudged the beautiful woman sitting by the king. She knows something he does not know. Within her is the knowledge that will bring about his death. It's just a matter of time. You never know how much is really occurring inside the minds of those around you.

Take a second look at the person others are despising. Remember Jesus at the crucifixion? Thousands are jeering. Look twice. His eyes are still focused. His voice is still clear. He is *the Son of God*. One thief on the cross next to Him looks again at Jesus, and enters Eternity forgiven. In minutes the thief will be with Him in Paradise. "And he said unto Jesus, Lord, remember me when Thou comest into Thy kingdom. And Jesus said...Today shalt thou be with Me in paradise" (Luke 23:42,43).

Look again at a situation you don't yet understand. Imagine Mary, the Virgin Mother of Jesus. See her huddled over on the small donkey? The blanket is covering a small child. The child is Jesus, the Son of God, Who will give His life for this world. She needs a place to sleep. Someone has the opportunity of a lifetime to bless the Son of God.

Look again at someone who appears out of place. Picture David, the teenage shepherd, talking to his soldier brothers on the battlefield. He has a slingshot. In minutes Goliath will fall dead at his feet. *The only thing between insignificance and fame was his enemy* (see 1 Samuel 17:41-51).

Look again at a helpless situation. Imagine the little boy in the crowd following Jesus. See him in the corner? Look again. His lunch basket contains five loaves and two fishes that will feed this entire crowd within the next 30 minutes (see John 6:8-13).

Look again at an unreasonable and illogical request. Imagine the scenario Joseph created with his brother in the palace. I can imagine the shock when Joseph told his brother to bring Benjamin to him. Look at this man again. He is giving you an instruction. Bring back your baby brother. He wants to see him face to face. Don't get angry. This man is the brother you wronged but mercy will flow from him *as you complete his instruction.* He is capable of providing for you and your family the rest of their lives. He's offering to do it. Follow his instruction (see Genesis 42:18-24).

Look again at an enemy that appears unchangeable. Imagine Saul the tormentor of the church. Note his passion. He is dead wrong, but he does not know it yet. The same Holy Spirit Who empowered you to preach today, Stephen, is looking at this man. God is about to throw him on the ground (give him a new heart) and make him blind for three days. That man holding the coats of those stoning you is only hours from a dramatic transformation. Soon he will become the apostle of apostles, the Apostle Paul! The man attacking your anointing is about to receive the same victory and breakthrough!

Look again at your empty bank account. Consider Peter the fisherman who has caught nothing for an entire night. You're tired. You're exhausted and angry. A man is talking to you. *Listen to him.* Lift your head up higher. He is giving you an instruction. Yes, you *already* understand fishing. But this man is telling you to do something *different* (see John 21:6).

Cast your net on the other side.

Listen to him, Mr. Bankrupt Fisherman. You are about to pull in the greatest net of fish you have ever caught in a single day. In fact, others will come over to help you. You are only 30 minutes away from the biggest financial increase you have ever experienced.

► Nobody is as they first appear.
► Nobody is going to stay the same as today.
► Anyone you know can experience a 180-degree *turn within* 24 hours from today.

God is looking at something in them *that you cannot see.* The Holy Spirit has been interceding for them. Jesus is interceding for them and helping them.

Remember, people are often greater than they first appear. God sees something in them *you* must discover. Keep reminding yourself of this.

This is One of the Secrets of Career Success.

≈ Matthew 5:7 ≈

"Blessed are the merciful: for they shall obtain mercy."

———≈•◦•≈———

❧ 19 ❧

ALWAYS ALLOW OTHERS ROOM TO TURN AROUND.

━━━━━◆❖◆━━━━━

Everybody Makes Mistakes.
Everybody deserves the chance to change.
Allow them to do so.

When pressure increases, those around you are affected and influenced. Their stress can affect you. The constant demands of others often birth impatience and mistakes. During these moments, *your mercy is necessary.*

Wrong words are often blurted out.

Inaccurate assessments are made.

Wrong decisions are made.

Think back upon your own life. Many frustrations drove you to that moment of indiscretion, those cutting words and angry outbursts.

Allow forgiveness.

Don't force others to live by their past bad decisions. Whatever you sow will come back to you a hundred times. So give them space to come back into the relationship *with dignity.* Jesus taught it. "Blessed are the merciful: for they shall obtain mercy" (Matthew 5:7).

Forgive them 490 times. "Then came Peter to Him, and said, Lord, how oft shall my brother sin against me, and I forgive him? till seven times? Jesus saith unto him, I say not unto thee, Until seven times: but, Until seventy times seven" (Matthew 18:21-22).

Forgive seventy times seven. Give them *enough* time. Things are happening you cannot see. Sometimes it takes weeks and even months for some to realize and admit their mistakes.

Give them a season of *solitude*.

Give them opportunities for *expression*, an opportunity to explain themselves. They may *not* know the right choice of words the *first time*. Be willing to *listen longer*.

Give them time to evaluate *every* part of the puzzle. You may be looking at one part. They are considering many different factors they have yet to discuss with you.

Give them time to discover the truth *about you*. You already know yourself. They do not. They do not know all of your *flaws*. They do not know all of your *capabilities*. They do not understand your *memories*. Your pain. Your goals or dreams.

They may be looking at now.

You are looking at tomorrow.

Allow others space to correct their mistakes.

It's One of the Secrets of Career Success.

≈ 20 ≈

Secure A Receipt For Everything.

Document Every Purchase.

Develop the habit of keeping receipts on everything you buy. When I leave the airport, I secure a receipt for the fifty cents it costs at parking. Not because I need the reimbursement, but I need the *habit* of asking for a receipt to be emphasized and kept permanent in my life.

I want the habit to become *instinctive*, not requiring my memory or attention.

Here Are 6 Benefits In Keeping Receipts

1. *The Habit Of Keeping Receipts Will Help You With Your Taxes.* When you complete your income tax forms at the end of the year, you'll be thankful for every receipt that can be deducted from your Income Tax Return.

2. *Keeping Receipts Keeps You Reminded Of Where Your Money Has Been Spent.* This is important. Expenses are usually much more than what you had originally planned for. It will help you in budgeting and planning ahead.

3. *When You Keep Receipts, You Send A Message Of Organization And Order.* You know

what you are talking about and it shows.

4. *When You Keep Receipts, You Increase The Confidence Of Others Toward You.* They will consider your opinion valuable on other matters as well.

5. *When An Employee Approaches His Boss For A Reimbursement Without A Receipt, This Sends A Damaged Message To Him.* Were they sloppy in organizing their receipts? Did they really *secure* a receipt? Did they actually spend the money? Do they not care about the finances of the business?

6. *Keeping Receipts Can Help Protect Your Reputation For Integrity.*

When you fail to keep receipts:

1. You portray sloppiness and disorder.

2. You cause others to *doubt* everything you say.

3. You *slow down* the reimbursement process.

4. You create a climate of *suspicion*.

5. You send a message of rebellion and stubbornness.

Something interesting happened to me many years ago. When I left a motel in Kentucky, I pulled out my credit card to pay for my personal telephone calls. (The host church always pays for the room and food. But, I always pay for the telephone calls, faxes or other items.) I was in a hurry to the airport. I placed the receipt in my little leather bag.

In those days, I would often minister several weeks of meetings before returning home. Receipts always piled up. After a few weeks, I always have a stack of receipts that I cannot begin to explain to anyone! Especially when I'm taking flights, shoving $5.00 bills in the hands of bellmen at the motel or the hands of a skycap at the airport. When I am busy making change and running through airports, receipts often become a blur. (Since then, I try to *write the description of the purchase on every receipt.* This triggers my memory two or three weeks later when reviewing it with my bookkeeper.)

Thirty days later, the telephone rang. I was in my little garage working at my desk. (My office was then in Houston, Texas.) It was my pastor friend from Kentucky. He sounded distant and rather cool. He plunged in without the normal pleasantries.

"Hello, Mike? I just wanted to know why you did not pay your own telephone calls here at the motel when you checked out?"

He did not even bother asking me if I had paid the hotel for the telephone bill or not. He addressed me fully confident that the motel staff had given him accurate information.

I was taken aback. In fact, I felt rather agitated that he had not sought an explanation from me *first.* (The telephone bill was not that high, anyhow.) But, I explained to him that I *had* paid my own telephone bill.

"Well, they have just charged the church for it again, if you did pay it." He actually sounded like he believed the hotel over *me!*

I asked him to hold the line for a few moments. I began to dig through my desk drawer. Miraculously, I found the receipt in a stack of receipts in my desk drawer. I pulled it and gave the details to him on the phone. Then, I made a copy and mailed it to him. (This was before the creation of fax machines! May God bless the man or woman who created the fax machine!) The point is, my receipt salvaged my reputation.

The answer is simple. *Always get a receipt.*

Solomon was meticulous about record keeping. Every single animal used in a meal in the palace was accounted for. "Be thou diligent to know the state of thy flocks, and look well to thy herds" (Proverbs 27:23). Why? "For riches are not for ever" (Proverbs 27:24a).

Successful people secure *receipts* for everything. *It's One of the Secrets of Career Success.*

❧ 21 ❧

VERIFY EVERY INSTRUCTION.

Confirm Everything.

I have marveled how so many have kept their jobs over the years. Few seem to *follow-through* on instructions given to them by their supervisors.

True, there are a few close to you who may have proven themselves over a long period of time. They understand you. They are diligent, aggressive and trustworthy. But my own experience is that there are *less than five people* in your life that you can count on to *fully complete an assigned task with excellence.*

4 Ways To Recognize An Undependable Employee

1. *They Do Not Keep Paper And Pen In Their Hand.* Never trust an employee who does not regularly carry paper and pen in their hand to follow through on something you've asked them to do. *Never.* They trust their memory and want you to trust it also.

2. *They Make No Attempt To Ever Reach For Paper And Pen To Document The Instruction.* They simply nod. They do not *write* it down. They do not

document it. They trust their memory. Bank on it —the instruction will be *forgotten* in their busyness.

3. *They Ask No Additional Questions About The Assignment Or Instruction*. Few instructions are complete at the beginning. They *should* be asking:

    a.   Is there a *deadline* on this?

    b.   When do you need a *report back* on the results of this telephone call?

    c.   Is there anything *additional* I should know about?

When additional questions are never asked, following an instruction given, *they're not giving any thought to it.*

4. They Always Reply, "I will *try* to get to that, sir." *Believe me, they won't get to it.* The very word *"try"* gives them away.

7 Things You Should Remember When You Delegate Instructions To Others

1. Communicate Clearly *The Importance* Of The Instruction.

2. Give The Instruction To *One Person* Only.

3. *Document The Date* You Gave The Instruction.

4. Require A Continuous *Progress Report.*

5. *Agree* Upon The Expected Deadline For The Completion Of The Task.

6. Never Give An Instruction To Someone *Incapable Of Completing It.*

7. Never *Assume* Your Instructions Have Been Completed. Follow through.

It's One of the Secrets of Career Success.

❧ 22 ❧

Always Close Doors Gently.

━━━━▶➢◗➋◗◖❮━━━━

Relationships Do Not Always Last Forever.

So, it is important to *exit* every Door of Friendship properly. You cannot enter the next season of your life with joy unless you exit your present season *correctly*.

Jesus finished His work on earth. He cried out from the cross, "It is finished!" Salvation was complete. Redemption had taken place. He had paid the price for the sins of man. Three days later, the resurrection would take place. He would return to the Father where He would make intercession for you and me. He finished *properly*—with the approval of the Father.

Solomon finished the temple. It was an incredible feat. Some value his temple today at over $500 billion dollars. He was respected, pursued and celebrated. He *completed* what he started.

Paul finished his race. He fought a good fight, kept his course and finished the race. He was a success in the eyes of God. He made his exit from his earthly ministry with grace, passion and dignity.

Your life is a collection of *Beginnings*.

It is also a collection of *Exits*.

You will not stay in your present job forever.

You will someday leave your present position. Your supervisor today could be another acquaintance in your life next year. Close the relationship with dignity.

8 Keys To Remember When A Relationship Is Ending

1. *Close Every Door Gently*. Do not slam Doors. Do not kick Doors. Do not yell at Doors. They are Doors *through which you may need to return again* in the future. The attitude of *your exit* determines if you can ever walk back through that Door again. "A soft answer turneth away wrath: but grievous words stir up anger," (Proverbs 15:1).

2. *Close Doors With Forgiveness*. Unforgiveness is poisonous. It is the cancer that will destroy you from within. Release others to God. Permit Him to do the penalizing or correcting. Like Joseph, recognize that the ultimate plan of God will bring your promotion (see Romans 8:28).

3. *Close The Doors With Kindness*. If your fianceé leaves you with cutting and bitter words, thank the Holy Spirit for salvaging you. Perhaps she was not your *Proverbs 31 Woman* after all. "...in her tongue is the law of kindness" (Proverbs 31:26b).

4. *Close Every Door With Promises Fulfilled*. Don't leave your job until you have finished *what you promised*. Complete every vow. *Whatever* the cost. Integrity is easy to test. Simply ask yourself: Did I fulfill my promise? (see Ecclesiastes 5:4,5).

When people lose you in the Forest of Words, apply this Principle of Vow Fulfillment. Forget the blaming, complaining and accusations. This principle reveals everything you need to know about another.

5. *Close Every Door With Integrity.* Few will do it. *People are rarely angry for the reason they tell you.* Employees rarely leave for the reason they explain. Much is never discussed. The trap of deception is deadly. It begins when you deceive *yourself*, then, those around you. Always be honest to others about *the reason* for the Doors closing. It is not necessary to give *every* detail. But it is important that the details you give are *accurate.*

6. *Close Every Door With Courage.* It is not always easy to close a Door that the Holy Spirit requires. So, closing that Door requires uncommon courage to face the future without that person. Remember the precious Holy Spirit will never leave you nor forsake you (see John 14:16). He opens Doors. He closes Doors. He is the Bridge to every person in your future.

7. *Close Every Door With Expectation Of Promotion.* "For promotion cometh neither from the east, nor from the west, nor from the south. But God is the judge: he putteth down one, and setteth up another," (Psalm 75:6,7).

8. *Close Every Door By The Timing Of The Holy Spirit.* Do not close it in a fit of anger. Do not close the Door because of a misunderstanding that erupts. Do not close it just because someone *recommends* that you exit. Know the timing of God (see Ecclesiastes 3:1-8).

A young man sat in my kitchen a few weeks ago. I was quite concerned. He wanted a position in my ministry. I asked him about his relationship with his previous boss, my pastor friend. He avoided the issue continually. In fact, I had to ask him the question four or five times before I got a partial answer. At the end of the conversation, he explained his financial dilemma. He had left a job before ever securing another one. I explained to him how foolish this was. If God were moving him, He would tell him the place he was to go.

When God told Elijah to leave the brook, Zarephath was scheduled (see 1 Kings 17).

When the Israelites left Egypt, Canaan was their determined destination (see Exodus 13).

God always brings you out of a place to bring you into another place. So, close every Door with God's timing. When you close Doors gently, news will travel. Good news.

That's One of the Golden Secrets of Career Success.

❧ 23 ❧

Respect And Protect The Schedule And Agenda Of Others.

━━━━━◆━━━━━

Respect The Responsibilities Of Another.

I had finished a two-day School of the Holy Spirit up north. It had been a glorious two days. The presence of God was so powerful. I loved being with my friends and partners, as always.

However, due to the airline schedule, I had to leave 30 minutes earlier than planned. Another minister was going to finish the session for me. Because of the airline schedule, two flights were necessary and would let me arrive at my destination approximately at 1:00 a.m. in the morning. My schedule was hectic. In fact, I would barely make the church where I was scheduled. So, I announced to everyone present that my plane schedule was tight. I would be unable to stay afterwards for any additional conversation.

Yet, as I was rushing toward the door with my briefcase, my associate by my side, five to seven people stopped me. Standing in front of me, they insisted that I autograph my books. Some insisted that I hear about an experience they had had.

Each one of them *totally ignored my own*

schedule. They had no concern whatsoever.

Did they love me? Not really. They loved *themselves.* Their only obsession was *to get something* they wanted, regardless of the toll it took on me. My needs meant nothing. My own schedule was unimportant to them.

The Holy Spirit is always offended by such insensitivity and uncaring for others, "...in honour preferring one another;" (Romans 12:10b).

Always make sure your time with someone is appropriate for their schedule (see Ecclesiastes 3:1-8).

Reject manipulating, intimidating, and abusive words. "You never take time for me" is simply an attempt to intimidate you. Statements like, "You *never* have time for me. You always have time for everyone else!" is *victim* vocabulary. This kind of person has no true regard for others. They are obsessed with themselves. You cannot give them enough time or attention to satisfy them.

Always mark those who show disregard and disrespect for your time, the most precious gift God gave you. If they do not respect your time, neither will they respect your Wisdom.

When You Honor the Schedule of Others, Favor Will Flow.

It's One of the Secrets of Career Success.

≈ 24 ≈

DRESS THE WAY YOU WANT TO FEEL INSTEAD OF HOW YOU ARE PRESENTLY FEELING.

Your Clothes Can Really Affect You.

I learned this many years ago. Sometimes, when I would first awaken, I would not be in the "mood" to dress up nice. So, I would put on some old casual clothes laying across the chair. Throughout the day, I *would continue to feel* the identical way I had felt when I first woke up—rather sloppy. The clothes I had put on *reinforced my early morning mood and attitude.*

6 Facts You Should Remember About Clothing And Your Personal Appearance

1. *Your Appearance Influences Your Own Emotions.* I have learned a lot since those early days. Sometimes, when I am really feeling in a "don't care mood," I proceed to put on a nice suit, clean shirt and attractive tie. Within minutes, my energy and mood *adapt* to my new appearance. I begin to feel

and become the way I am dressed.

2. *Your Clothes Send A Message To Others.*
The Proverbs 31 woman dressed to communicate her
dignity. "She maketh herself coverings of tapestry;
her clothing *is* silk and purple," (Proverbs 31:22).

3. *Your Clothing Educates Others In How You
Desire To Be Approached.* That's why the prostitute
dressed to seduce a man. "And, behold, there met
him a woman *with* the attire of an harlot, and subtle
of heart," (Proverbs 7:10).

4. *Your Clothes Influence What Others Feel
Toward You.* That's why Joseph shaved his beard
and changed his raiment when he came into the court
of Pharaoh. Egyptians hated beards. Joseph
packaged himself for where he was going instead of
where he had been.

5. *Your Clothes Can Create A Climate Of
Acceptance Or Rejection.* That's why Joseph *changed*
his outward appearance to create a climate of
acceptance (read Genesis 41:14).

6. *Your Clothes Can Influence The Decisions
And Plans Of Those Who See You.* Naomi mentored
Ruth about her dress and appearance. When she
approached Boaz, she made herself *desirable* for the
man she desired (Ruth 4:1).

Dress to create the feeling you need for the job
you face.

Dress The Way You Want To Feel, Instead Of
How You Are Presently Feeling.

That's One of the Secrets of Career Success.

❧ 25 ❧

Always Keep A Small Tape Recorder In Your Hand.

Talking Is Faster Than Writing.

Someone has said that you can talk six times faster than you can write. I *always* keep note paper and pen handy. *Always*. But, it is far easier and more productive to dictate into a little tape recorder than it is to write longhand on my legal pad. (Admittedly, some of my handwritten notes excite me more when I can *see* them written large in my own handwriting using a black pen.) But, when there is a flood of ideas and thoughts pouring through me, I consider the small tape recorder to be a gift from God. Every achiever should own and *use* one.

I have only known two friends in my entire life who keep a microcassette recorder with them at all times. Others claim to have them "somewhere in my office." Or somewhere "down here in my briefcase." But, they are not accustomed to thinking or using a recorder on a continuous basis.

Recording frees your mind from the stress of memory. When you want to remember something, you may find yourself continuously replaying it over and over in your mind, so you will not forget it.

Consequently, your mind cannot be free for conversation, a great *idea or* a season of unusual creativity. Why? Because subconsciously you are trying to *remember* something you need to do or tell someone else.

We try everything to help us remember. We keep lists, tie strings around our fingers, post notes. But, when you create the habit of keeping a microcassette recorder with you *every moment* of your life, you will began to produce ten times more than ever before. It has worked for me!

Develop the habit of keeping your recorder conveniently close. It may be uncomfortable, initially. When I first started keeping my microcassette in my pocket, it seemed a little odd and awkward, even cumbersome. However, once I saw the many pages of material the habit produced, it became a joy. This wonderful tool was a constant reminder that great thoughts and ideas were flowing through me all day.

Making your moments productive is one of the greatest Secrets of Life. Thousands keep waiting for a time that they are going to take off a few days or weeks and produce a book, plan a project or design their house. Fifty years can go by without any of it ever occurring, unless you understand how to *turn each moment into a miracle.*

Use your recorder daily.

Always Keep A Small Tape Recorder In Your Hand.

That is One of the most important Golden Secrets of Career Success you can learn.

∼ 26 ∼

Invest Whatever Is Necessary To Create The Atmosphere That Motivates You.

―――❖❖❖―――

Your Chosen Focus Requires A Unique Climate. Your surroundings are so important. Your atmosphere must receive your attention. It will not happen automatically. You must control the atmosphere around your life or it will control you.

16 Keys In Creating The Climate And Atmosphere You Need

1. *Your Climate Influences The Decisions You Make.* When you are in a high fashion clothing store, the music is often quiet, classical, or dignified. When you go into a store where the younger generation makes purchases, the music is fast, upbeat, and energizing. The merchants have created an environment that influences you to buy.

2. *Your Surroundings Contain Colors That Affect You Emotionally.* Many years ago, I read where a certain shade of pink was used in prisons to reduce violence and fights. Some say that

bodybuilders can lose one third of their ability if they look at a pink wall while they work out. Colors affect us. Colors affect our strength, our enthusiasm and the decisions we make.

3. *Everyone Needs Something Different Around Them.* You must discern what environment and atmosphere brings out the best in you.

When I need energy and must move quickly from project to project, I love to listen to praise music that is *energizing* and exciting. When I want to ponder and reflect, I love to listen to slower, more worshipful music. I know the value of *protecting the climate* around myself.

4. *Nobody Else Can Create Your Atmosphere For You.* You must discern it and pursue it for yourself.

5. *Nobody Else Really Cares About Your Specific Needs Like You Do.* So, do not wait and hope someone emerges who will take an aggressive part in making it happen for you.

6. *Nobody Else Is Responsible For Providing You With The Climate You Desire.* It is *your* life, *your* needs, and *your* decisions.

7. *You Will Not Do Your Very Best Until Everything Around You Is In Place.* Yes, you may achieve and be productive to a degree. But, you can multiply the results of your life when the things around you strengthen and motivate you.

8. *What You See Controls What You Desire.* When you see a billboard advertising hamburgers, you suddenly receive a desire for hamburgers. That's why you must put *around* yourself pictures and images of the things you want.

9. *What You Are Viewing Daily Affects What You Desire To Do.* When children see the playground

at McDonald's, they are suddenly inspired to stop everything and go play.

10. *Keep Around You Photographs Of Things You Want In Your Future.* It may be a boat you want to buy, a home you want to live in or a picture of yourself 20 pounds lighter. These images are influencing *the direction* your decisions will take you.

11. *Your Environment Is Worth Any Investment In Music And Equipment.* Buy a stereo or whatever it takes—get the *best* possible.

Every morning, I listen to the Scriptures on cassette tape. That's the first thing I do each day. Yes, they cost. The cassette recorder costs. But, my future and my emotions are worth any investment.

I purchase candles that smell the best, strongest and last the longest. Placing them around my room helps provide the most incredible atmosphere of reflection, warmth and caring. I need that. My heart requires it. If I do not do it, it will not be done. So, because it is *my* life that is so vital to me, I invest *whatever is necessary.*

A few days ago, I spent over $100 on several CD's. Yet, when I purchased them, I really was not just purchasing some music on compact disks. *I was purchasing an atmosphere.*

You see, this morning, after listening to the Bible on tape, I turned the CD player on. On the six CD's were birds, a sparkling, flowing fountain and peaceful music. Within seconds, I felt like I was under the trees alone and quiet, tasting the richness of God's nature around me. Yet, I was in my *bedroom!* I did not have to spend $2,000 to take a vacation to Honolulu. I simply needed an investment in my atmosphere—the appropriate CD's.

12. *Your Investment In Interior Decorating Can*

Make A Huge Difference In Your Productivity. A new rug, a picture on the wall, a vase with a rose, every small thing can increase the warmth and caring of your environment.

13. *Invest The Effort And Experimentation To Discover What You Really Need Around You.* That's all right, too. It's wonderful to explore variations of climates and environments. An interior decorator, the suggestions of a friend or your own personal visits to different stores can help you discover the atmosphere you prefer to work in, play around or simply relax and rest in. Each atmosphere produces a different emotion.

14. *Don't Wait On Others To Initiate Changes In Your Environment.* Make any investment necessary to create the kind of environment that inspires you toward excellence and the improvement of your life.

15. *Your Atmosphere Can Often Determine Your Productivity.* Many businesses have discovered an increase in unity and employee morale when they played music quietly throughout the offices. Many business corporations invest thousands of dollars to place signs of encouragement and motivation on the walls of their offices.

Why?

16. *What You See Affects The Decisions You Are Making.* It doesn't cost you a fortune to create a *favorable* atmosphere. Just think, look around and ask questions. Explore a little. Experiment.

Invest Whatever Is Necessary To Create The Atmosphere You Want To Surround You.

It's One of the Secrets of Career Success.

❧ 27 ❧

WALK ONE HOUR A DAY.

➤◦◄

Walking Produces Incredible Results.

Several years ago, I met a dynamic young lady who was a remarkable singer. She lived in California. She worked some for my company, Win-Song Productions. When I shared with her my desire to become physically fit, she really encouraged me.

Later, when she flew into Dallas, she would talk enthusiastically about us taking walks. So, I began with two or three miles at a time. She danced cheerfully up the road in front of me while I "waddled" my 200 plus pounds slowly along. Within a few days, however, my entire outlook had changed. My *enthusiasm* for everything *multiplied*. I felt warmer toward people and more precise in my focus. I became a different person in every aspect. The results were powerful and positive.

Soon, I was able to run five miles without stopping. This was a miracle for me. Those were marvelous and incredible days of energy and joy. *Ideas* flourished. Guilt over weight and stress because of procrastination left me. I was on schedule. I was doing the right things at the right time.

10 Steps Towards Better Health. Here's What I Learned

1. *Nobody Else Could Exercise For Me.* Yes, they could sit around discussing it at supper. I could

look at magazines and envy those who did. Or, I could focus on my personal need to get fit and get involved.

2. *Few Could Actually Encourage Me Effectively.* Some wanted to encourage me, but due to their own inability to encourage themselves, their words had no impact or effectiveness. You see, it's hard for someone that never exercises themselves to really get you enthused over it.

3. *Everyone Seems To Be In A Conspiracy To Weaken Your Resolve For Maximum Health.* When I would say "No thank you," to a dessert, my entire table of friends would turn on me like I had leprosy. "Of course, you can. This small bite won't hurt you!"

Another said, "You don't look bad. You deserve some dessert."

Unfortunately, many of my friends have little interest in maximized health. It has been a lonely road. Stopping desserts from being served to me after services has often caused a real stir. (Our obsession for food is unexplainable.) At conferences, churches have posters throughout their complex encouraging everyone: "Excellence...we are into excellence!" Then, you go to the pastor's office where platters of donuts, cakes and cookies are served. When I beg off, disappointment often emerges.

One pastor explained, "Mike, our ladies have waited all year for this conference. It would hurt them if you do not eat some of the things they worked so hard to prepare." Do not expect everyone to help in your pursuit of uncommon health.

4. *You Must Become Militant About Your Health.* Go on the offensive. If you don't, you will be pulled down by everybody around you. Name your friends who exercise daily, eat properly and

encourage you to do the same. How many are there? Two? Three? Probably none.

5. *Focus On The Results Of Your Walking, Instead Of The Walking.* Your guilt will vanish over your laziness. Walking is proof that you are not lazy. Your mind will free up miraculously. Your greatest ideas will flourish.

6. *Keep A Microcassette Recorder With You For Special Dictation When You Walk.* Ideas will flourish when you walk.

7. *Use Headphones And Listen To The Teaching Tapes You Have Been Wanting To Listen To For A Long Time.* Walking can become your personal mentorship hour.

8. *Invite A Friend Or Protégé Who Has Been Requesting Quality Time With You To Walk With You.*

9. *Keep Scripture Cards For Memorizing A New Verse Daily.* Your daily walk can become your Bible memorization period, teaching tape session or dictation moment. Several wonderful things can happen simultaneously.

10. *Document The Benefits Of Your Walking.* Moving toward tasks becomes easier. Your breathing will improve. You will be able to tell the difference in your conversations and in your health. Your self confidence will grow. You will no longer be plagued by guilt about neglecting your health.

Walking is the Habit of Champions. Harry Truman, at age eighty, continued to walk an hour a day to the end of his life. J. Don George, my longtime pastor friend here in Dallas, told me once, "Running solves problems. One of the most wonderful things about it is I don't have to watch what I eat as much." (I have been amazed at the food manipulations I will go through to *avoid exercising!*)

Those who insist that a little extra dessert won't hurt you are either ignorant or uncaring. It is not about a little piece of cake. It concerns a *life-style of habit. When you break a good habit, it takes more than you can imagine to ever rebuild again.*

Here Are 5 Additional Health Habits That Will Help You Lose Weight And Aid You Toward Uncommon Health

1. *Drink Water Consistently*. Loads of it. Put a gallon of water in front of you on the table where you work. Focus on emptying it that day. The results will amaze you.

2. *Keep A Plate Of Fruit Or Carrots And Celery Sticks By Your Bed*. Make that your midnight snack instead of cookies. Build the habit of long-term healthy eating.

3. *Ask Quality Friends To Encourage You*. Be honest about the passion of your heart, about your desire for uncommon health. Tell them you really want their help.

4. *Ask The Holy Spirit To Enable You To Take Steps In The Right Direction, Every Day.*

5. *Visualize Your Body As The Temple Of The Holy Spirit*. It pleases God immeasurably when you give attention to the temple He inhabits.

Wake yourself up, or someday the *doctor's report* will wake you up in the emergency room.

Walk One Hour A Day.

It is One of the Secrets of Career Success.

❧ 28 ❧

ESTABLISH YOUR PERSONAL SECRET PLACE OF PRAYER DAILY.

⟫-◈-⟪

The Secret Place Is The Place Where You Meet With God Every Day Of Your Life.

It is where you enter His presence and become changed, informed, corrected, and loved. It is the room where you kneel in humility at the altar of mercy and receive forgiveness, restoration, and revelation regarding your Assignment on earth.

It is your prayer room, the prayer closet, or *any place* you have sanctified and set apart for the *exclusive use of the Holy Spirit* to deal privately and intimately with your life.

This focus on *The Secret Place* is possibly the most life changing, revolutionizing teaching you may hear during your lifetime, if you discern the dramatic encounters such a place can birth.

15 Keys For Entering Your Secret Place Of Prayer

1. *Enter Daily.* The Psalmist said, "Lord, I have called daily upon Thee, I have stretched out my hands unto Thee" (Psalm 88:9b).

2.   *Enter With Expectation.* God honors it. "...for he that cometh to God must believe that He is, and *that* He is a rewarder of them that diligently seek Him" (Hebrews 11:6b).

Expectation is a current. It sweeps you into the Holy Place. It brings you into God's presence where you are purged, purified and changed.

▶ Expect God to *respond* to you.

▶ Expect pain to *leave* your body.

▶ Expect *confusion* to depart from your mind.

▶ Expect *revelation* concerning those you love to come to you.

▶ Expect *change* when you enter God's presence.

▶ Expect supernatural *peace* and joy to explode within your heart as you enter His presence.

3.   *Enter Before Making Financial Decisions.* The Apostle Paul understood this. "But my God shall supply all your need according to His riches in glory by Christ Jesus" (Philippians 4:19).

4.   *Enter Confessing Your Weaknesses And Expect To Be Made Strong.* Jesus is your difference. "I can do all things through Christ which strengtheneth me" (Philippians 4:13).

5.   *Enter With A Broken And Contrite Spirit.* Humility is the magnet that never fails to attract God. "The Lord *is* nigh unto them that are of a broken heart; and saveth such as be of a contrite spirit" (Psalm 34:18).

6.   *Enter When You Feel Forsaken And All Alone.* It worked for the greatest king of Israel. "I have been young, and now am old; yet have I not

seen the righteous forsaken, nor His seed begging bread" (Psalm 37:25).

7. *Enter When You Need Mercy.* It was the secret of David's *anointing.* "*He is* ever merciful" (Psalm 37:26a).

8. *Enter When You Have Fallen Into Deep Sin And Erred.* Reaching is your remedy for sins (read Psalm 37:23,24).

9. *Enter When Slanderous Words Are Stirring Up Enemies And Strife Against You.* The arms of God are always your best defense. "Thou shalt hide them in the secret of Thy presence from the pride of man: Thou shalt keep them secretly in a pavilion from the strife of tongues" (Psalm 31:20).

10. *Enter During Seasons Of Confusion And Change.* Transition is often your most vulnerable season. "My times *are* in Thy hand: deliver me from the hand of mine enemies, and from them that persecute me" (Psalm 31:15).

11. *Enter When You Are Divided In Your Decision Making And Do Not Know Which Road To Take.* Consulting God is never a mistake. "I will instruct thee and teach thee in the way which thou shalt go: I will guide thee with Mine eye" (Psalm 32:8).

12. *Enter When Bankruptcy Threatens And Poverty Is Strangling You Financially.* God wants you to prosper. "This poor man cried, and the Lord heard *him,* and saved him out of all his troubles" (Psalm 34:6).

13. *Enter Into The Secret Place When You Are Threatened, Abused, Or Afraid.* "The angel of the Lord encampeth round about them that fear Him,

and delivereth them" (Psalm 34:7).

14. *Enter Into His Presence When It Appears That Your Dreams And Goals Are Unachievable.* God loves the impossible. "O fear the Lord ye His saints: for *there is* no want to them that fear Him. The young lions do lack, and suffer hunger: but they that seek the Lord shall not want any good *thing*" (Psalm 34:9,10).

15. *Enter Into His Presence When Everything Is Going Well And Perfect In Your Life.* The goodness of God deserves recognition. "I will bless the Lord at all times: His praise *shall* continually *be* in my mouth. My soul shall make her boast in the Lord:" (Psalm 34:2a).

Establish Your Personal Secret Place For Meeting Daily With The Holy Spirit.

It is One of the Secrets of Career Success.

∼ 29 ∼

PINPOINT YOUR GREATEST GOALS.

Few Know What They Really Want To Do.
That is why they change their entire plan for the day when a friend drops by the house. Their goals were not clear. They really were not sold on their goals for that day.

7 Facts About Your Dreams And Goals

1. *Nobody Can Determine Your Own Goals For You.* You must decide what generates joy in your own heart.
2. *Different People Have Different Goals.* What is important to me may be totally unimportant to another. When they get in my presence, the difference emerges.
Let me explain.
I have a dream of creating a ten-year Mentorship Program for Parents. This consists of 120 extraordinary books. Using a chapter each day (31 keys for each 31 days of the month), I would like to create a mentorship system for parents to use with their children ages six years old to sixteen years old.
This would provide parents with a "Wisdom Encyclopedia" for their family. At breakfast, each

morning, they could read one chapter and mentor their children on such topics as: 31 Facts About God, 31 Facts About Jesus, 31 Facts About The Holy Spirit, 31 Facts About Angels, 31 Facts About Achieving Your Dream, 31 Reasons Why People Do Not Receive Their Financial Harvest and so forth.

Personally, I have a plan for every day of my life. Every moment of my life.

When I am tired or need a change, I stop the plan and do something different for recreation for a couple of hours. But, I am very positive about what I want to do with my life.

But, I have some friends who do not have any drive or passion to accomplish anything. Their goal is to pay their bills for the month. So, after they get paid, and they want to "have fun," they drop by my office. They want to talk. You see, they do not really respect the dreams of others. My goal is not vital to them. In fact, they usually want to preach me a sermon on how I need to "relax." I am relaxed. I am happy. I do not need them in my life for relaxation. Sometimes these friends are a distraction. That is why you must pinpoint your own goals.

3.   *Do Not Depend On Others To Inspire You Regarding Your Dreams.* Most will distract you. They do not value what you are pursuing. They do not celebrate what you are pursuing. You must name it for what it really is and move on with your life.

4.   *You Must Determine What Your Goals Are Financially, Spiritually, Or Physically.* Others cannot borrow your goals for themselves. You may have wonderful goals for those you love, but if they do not have the same dream for themselves, it is a waste of

your time and energy.

Some years ago I purchased a special little building for a physical fitness center for my staff. I was so excited. I hired a trainer to help each of my people develop their maximum level of health. It lasted less than a month. At the end of three weeks, only two people would show up at the special meeting with the trainer that was costing me $75 an hour. I was paying the trainer for them. But, they simply did not have any personal goals for themselves. The equipment was wasted. You simply cannot make others pursue worthwhile dreams for themselves.

5. *Avoid Intimate Relationships With People Who Disrespect Your Dreams.* You can minister to them. You can encourage them. You can speak words that will strengthen and bless them. But, do not draw them close in or the burden will become too cumbersome and impossible for you to carry.

6. *Put Pictures Of Your Goals And Dreams On Your Walls In Your Office, In Your Secret Place And On Your Refrigerator.* If you have a dream of losing weight, put pictures in front of you that inspire and excite you. Do you have a dream of owning your own home? Place a picture of it on the bulletin board at your home. What you keep looking at the most will influence your conversation and your faith.

7. *Write Out Your Dream On Paper.* "...Write the vision, and make *it* plain upon tables, that he may run that readeth it" (Habakkuk 2:2b). A thought is not a plan. A wish is not a plan. A possibility is not a plan. True champions invest time and energy to develop a clear-cut written goal and dream. They plan for their life.

Always Pinpoint Your Goals.
It's One of the Golden Secrets of Career Success.

≈ 30 ≈

Always See Rejection As A Door, Not A Wall.

Rejection Is A Beginning, Not An End.

It is merely someone's opinion. Someone who is incapable of discerning your greatness.

Look at Walt Disney. Millions have enjoyed the incredible entertainment he has provided through Disney World. Who has been more creative on this earth than Walt Disney? But, there was a time in his life that his climate and situation did not inspire him. He was once fired by a newspaper because they felt he was "not creative enough." He knew rejection. They did not want him. He lost a job because of the opinions of others.

Yet, Disney saw rejection *as a door* to his next season. It was not a wall. It was not a conclusion. It was the entry into change.

Your loved ones may reject you. In his tremendous book, "The Salesman of the Century," Ron Popeil shares an encouraging note. His success is widely known. He has made millions in his presentations of inventions on television. Yet, he experienced feeling unloved. He writes, "Even though over the years I helped to make my father a richer man by selling his products on television, I still never got close to him. He never said he loved me...I never heard the word love from any of my relatives" (page 41). You see, he saw past their problem. He saw past their harshness. He *saw his future.*

Rejection cannot stop your future from emerging. Your unwillingness to persist can stop your future. Make up your mind today to overcome every rejection you have experienced during your lifetime. Learn from it. Focus on something bigger than the opinions of others—your future success.

Your gifts and labors may be rejected. A number of years ago, Richard Bach wrote a ten thousand word story about a soaring seagull.

It was turned down by 18 publishers.

Finally, MacMillan published it in 1970. Within five years, by 1975, Jonathan Livingston Seagull had sold more than seven million copies in the United States alone.

Seven million copies after 18 rejections.

The opinions of others have nothing to do with your success. Their rejection can only affect your feelings, not your future.

What you discuss with others will become bigger. What you think about will multiply. Stop telling about your rejections. *Feed your dream until it becomes so big you cannot remember the rejection.*

Insist on overcoming rejection.

Always See Rejection As A Door, Not A Wall.

It's One of the Secrets of Career Success.

∾ 31 ∾

REMIND YOURSELF CONTINUOUSLY THAT OTHERS NEAR YOU ARE HURTING INSIDE.

Everyone Is Hiding Something.

It is not always because of deception. Neither are they trying to cover up something important.

Our wounds are simply private.

The things that make us cry often embarrass us. When a wife has received a harsh look from her husband, the pain goes too deep to discuss. When the husband hears the acid words from the love of his life, he comes apart *inside*. Yet, he cannot afford to show it. Neither can she. Nobody wants to look weak. So, every effort is made to shield ourselves, protect ourselves from the prying and often critical opinions of others.

So, nobody really sees how much *you hurt*.

I try to remind myself of this continuously. I fail a lot in it. Sometimes, if someone seems a little arrogant and aggressive, I will tend to confront them on that turf. I do not mind confrontation, since I think I am right most of the time! (Smile!) But, they are thinking *they* are right also!

Here is the problem.

You do not *really* know what is going on in another person's mind, therefore, it is important to continuously remind yourself that *others have painful experiences that they are not discussing with you or anyone else.*

Their decisions about everything are being made to *avoid the continuance* of that pain, thus repeating their failures. So, they will not make decisions totally based on what you are saying, your conversations. They are making decisions to move away from pain.

Every decision is to move away from anticipated pain. Every decision is presumed to be an escape to pleasure, away from that pain.

When I remind myself of this, I am more gentle with people. More understanding. Less critical and harsh. Far more patient than I would normally be. You see, I want people to be patient with me too.

One of the secrets of the journey is to continuously, *continuously* remind yourself that others are going *through trials you cannot see.*

They are crying tears you have never felt.

They are feeling isolated and rejected in ways you cannot imagine.

Do not become *another* burden to them.

Become *their Burden Bearer.*

When you telephone someone, ask yourself, "Am I calling to add to their burden *or to remove it?*"

When you write a letter, ask yourself, "Am I becoming *another* burden or their Burden Bearer?"

Maturity is the ability and willingness to bear the burdens of others.

Many years ago, I was in Fullerton, California.

The church was full of people. But, the service seemed very uptight and tense. Something was wrong. I almost became belligerent and told the people something every young evangelist normally tells the people.

"If you don't like what I'm preaching, stay home. The door swings both ways. I don't have to be here myself. I can leave town if I want to. I'm going to preach this gospel...no matter what you say. I'd rather preach under a tree by myself, than compromise this gospel." (Blah. Blah. Blah.)

But, Someone restrained me. (The Holy Spirit!)

After church, I discovered the reason for the terrible deathly atmosphere of the service. One of the main board members of the church had suddenly dropped dead that afternoon. Yet, his entire family had chosen to come sit in the service that night rather than go to the funeral home. They were so desperate for God to speak a word of comfort and strength to them, they came to the crusade.

Had I said what I felt—I would have doubled their pain and heartache. *Someone is always going through something you have not discerned.*

Listen to the Holy Spirit. Become intuitive. *Nothing is ever as it first appears.*

Why did I remain composed and focused during the service, even though the church atmosphere was like death? I remembered *reading* a statement by a great preacher. He said every young preacher *"should always remember that on every pew sits at least one broken heart. Heal it."*

You will meet many people today. Many need kind words desperately.

Everyone hurts somewhere inside.

Most will not tell you about it. So, wrap your words with healing oil. You are their healer, sent by God.

You may be the only healer that crosses their path during their lifetime.

When you concentrate on the needs of others, God will focus on *your* needs. "Knowing that whatsoever good thing any man doeth, the same shall he receive of the Lord, whether *he be* bond or free" (Ephesians 6:8).

Remind Yourself Continuously That Others Near You Are Hurting Inside.

That's One of the Secrets of Career Success.

DECISION

Will You Accept Jesus As Your Personal Savior Today?

The Bible says, "That if thou shalt confess with thy mouth the Lord Jesus, and shalt believe in thine heart that God hath raised Him from the dead, thou shalt be saved" (Rom. 10:9).

Pray this prayer from your heart today!

"Dear Jesus, I believe that You died for me and rose again on the third day. I confess I am a sinner...I need Your love and forgiveness... Come into my heart. Forgive my sins. I receive your eternal life. Confirm Your love by giving me peace, joy and supernatural love for others. Amen."

Clip and Mail

DR. MIKE MURDOCK

is in tremendous demand as one of the most dynamic speakers in America today.

More than 14,000 audiences in 38 countries have attended his meetings and seminars. Hundreds of invitations come to him from churches, colleges and business corporations. He is a noted author of over 120 books, including the best sellers, *"The Leadership Secrets of Jesus"* and *"Secrets of the Richest Man Who Ever Lived."* Thousands view his weekly television program, *"Wisdom Keys with Mike Murdock."* Many attend his Saturday School of Wisdom Breakfasts that he hosts in major cities of America.

☐ Yes, Mike! I made a decision to accept Christ as my personal Savior today. Please send me my free gift of your book, *"31 Keys to a New Beginning"* to help me with my new life in Christ. *(B-48)*

NAME _____ BIRTHDAY _____

ADDRESS _____

CITY _____ STATE ____ ZIP ____

PHONE _____ E-MAIL _____ *B-44*

Mail form to:
The Wisdom Center • P. O. Box 99 • Denton, TX 76202
Phone: 1-888-WISDOM-1 (1-888-947-3661)
*Website: **www.thewisdomcenter.cc***

113

ORDER FORM THE WISDOM CENTER
(All books paperback unless indicated otherwise.)

Qty	Code	Book Title	USA	Total
	B-01	Wisdom for Winning	$10	
	B-02	Five Steps Out of Depression	$ 3	
	B-03	The Sex Trap	$ 3	
	B-04	Ten Lies People Believe About Money	$ 3	
	B-05	Finding Your Purpose in Life	$ 3	
	B-06	Creating Tomorrow Through Seed-Faith	$ 3	
	B-07	Battle Techniques for War Weary Saints	$ 3	
	B-08	Enjoying the Winning Life	$ 3	
	B-09	Four Forces/Guarantee Career Success	$ 3	
	B-10	The Bridge Called Divorce	$ 3	
	B-11	Dream Seeds	$ 9	
	B-12	The Ministers Encyclopedia, Vol. 1	$20	
	B-13	Seeds of Wisdom on Dreams and Goals, Vol. 1	$ 3	
	B-14	Seeds of Wisdom on Relationships, Vol. 2	$ 3	
	B-15	Seeds of Wisdom on Miracles, Vol. 3	$ 3	
	B-16	Seeds of Wisdom on Seed-Faith, Vol. 4	$ 3	
	B-17	Seeds of Wisdom on Overcoming, Vol. 5	$ 3	
	B-18	Seeds of Wisdom on Habits, Vol. 6	$ 3	
	B-19	Seeds of Wisdom on Warfare, Vol. 7	$ 3	
	B-20	Seeds of Wisdom on Obedience, Vol. 8	$ 3	
	B-21	Seeds of Wisdom on Adversity, Vol. 9	$ 3	
	B-22	Seeds of Wisdom on Prosperity, Vol. 10	$ 3	
	B-23	Seeds of Wisdom on Prayer, Vol. 11	$ 3	
	B-24	Seeds of Wisdom on Faith-Talk, Vol. 12	$ 3	
	B-25	7 Kinds of People You Cannot Help	$ 5	
	B-26	The God Book	$10	
	B-27	The Jesus Book	$10	
	B-28	The Blessing Bible	$10	
	B-29	The Survival Bible	$10	
	B-30	The Teens Topical Bible	$ 7	
	B-31	Seeds of Wisdom Topical Bible	$15	
	B-32	The Ministers Topical Bible	$ 7	
	B-33	The Businessmans Topical Bible	$ 7	
	B-34	The Grandparents Topical Bible	$ 7	
	B-35	The Fathers Topical Bible	$ 7	
	B-36	The Mothers Topical Bible	$ 7	
	B-37	The New Converts Bible	$ 7	
	B-38	The Widows Topical Bible	$ 7	
	B-39	The Double Diamond Principle	$10	
	B-40	Wisdom for Crisis Times	$ 9	
	B-41	The Gift of Wisdom, Vol. 1	$10	
	B-42	1-Minute Businessmans Devotional	$12	
	B-43	1-Minute Businesswomans Devotional	$12	
	B-44	31 Secrets for Career Success	$10	
	B-45	101 Wisdom Keys	$ 5	
	B-46	31 Facts About Wisdom	$ 5	
	B-47	The Covenant of Fifty-Eight Blessings	$ 8	
	B-48	31 Keys to a New Beginning	$ 5	
	B-49	The Proverbs 31 Woman	$ 7	
	B-50	One-Minute Pocket Bible for the Achiever	$ 5	
	B-51	One-Minute Pocket Bible for Fathers	$ 5	
	B-52	One-Minute Pocket Bible for Mothers	$ 5	
	B-53	One-Minute Pocket Bible for Teenagers	$ 5	
	B-54	The Seeds of Wisdom Daily Devotional	$ 5	
	B-55	20 Keys to a Happier Marriage	$ 3	
	B-56	How to Turn Mistakes into Miracles	$ 3	

Qty	Code	Book Title	USA	Total
	B-57	31 Secrets of an Unforgettable Woman	$10	
	B-58	The Mentors Manna on Attitude	$ 3	
	B-59	The Making of a Champion	$ 5	
	B-60	One-Minute Pocket Bible for Men	$ 5	
	B-61	One-Minute Pocket Bible for Women	$ 5	
	B-62	One-Minute Pocket Bible/Bus.Professionals	$ 5	
	B-63	One-Minute Pocket Bible for Truckers	$ 5	
	B-64	Seven Obstacles to Abundant Success	$ 3	
	B-65	Born to Taste the Grapes	$ 3	
	B-66	Greed, Gold and Giving	$ 3	
	B-67	Gift of Wisdom for Champions	$10	
	B-68	Gift of Wisdom for Achievers	$10	
	B-69	Wisdom Keys for a Powerful Prayer Life	$ 3	
	B-70	Gift of Wisdom for Mothers	$10	
	B-71	Wisdom - God's Golden Key to Success	$ 7	
	B-72	The Double Diamond Daily Devotional	$15	
	B-73	The Mentors Manna on Abilities	$ 3	
	B-74	The Assignment: Dream/Destiny, Vol. 1	$10	
	B-75	The Assignment: Anointing/Adversity, Vol. 2	$10	
	B-76	The Mentors Manna on Assignment	$ 3	
	B-77	The Gift of Wisdom for Fathers	$10	
	B-78	The Mentors Manna on the Secret Place	$ 3	
	B-79	The Mentors Manna on Achievement	$ 3	
	B-80	The Greatest Success Habit on Earth	$ 3	
	B-81	The Mentors Manna on Adversity	$ 3	
	B-82	31 Reasons People Do Not Receive Their Financial Harvest	$12	
	B-83	The Gift of Wisdom for Wives	$10	
	B-84	The Gift of Wisdom for Husbands	$10	
	B-85	The Gift of Wisdom for Teenagers	$10	
	B-86	The Gift of Wisdom for Leaders	$10	
	B-87	The Gift of Wisdom for Graduates	$10	
	B-88	The Gift of Wisdom for Brides	$10	
	B-89	The Gift of Wisdom for Grooms	$10	
	B-90	The Gift of Wisdom for Ministers	$10	
	B-91	The Leadership Secrets of Jesus	$10	
	B-92	Secrets of the Journey, Vol. 1	$ 5	
	B-93	Secrets of the Journey, Vol. 2	$ 5	
	B-94	Secrets of the Journey, Vol. 3	$ 5	
	B-95	Secrets of the Journey, Vol. 4	$ 5	
	B-96	Secrets of the Journey, Vol. 5	$ 5	
	B-97	The Assignment: Trials/Triumphs, Vol. 3	$ 5	
	B-98	The Assignment: Pain/Passion, Vol. 4	$ 5	
	B-99	Secrets of the Richest Man Who Ever Lived	$10	
	B-100	The Holy Spirit Handbook, Vol. 1	$10	
	B-101	The 3 Most Important Things in Your Life	$10	
	B-102	Secrets of the Journey, Vol. 6	$ 5	
	B-103	Secrets of the Journey, Vol. 7	$ 5	
	B-104	7 Keys to 1000 Times More	$10	
	B-105	31 Keys for Succeeding on Your Job	$10	
	B-106	The Uncommon Leader	$ 5	
	B-107	The Uncommon Minister, Vol. 1	$ 5	
	B-108	The Uncommon Minister, Vol. 2	$ 5	
	B-109	The Uncommon Minister, Vol. 3	$ 5	
	B-110	The Uncommon Minister, Vol. 4	$ 5	
	B-111	The Uncommon Minister, Vol. 5	$ 5	
	B-112	The Uncommon Minister, Vol. 6	$ 5	
	B-113	The Uncommon Minister, Vol. 7	$ 5	

Qty	Code	Book Title	USA	Total
	B-114	The Law of Recognition	$10	
	B-115	Seeds of Wisdom on The Secret Place, Vol. 13	$ 5	
	B-116	Seeds of Wisdom on The Holy Spirit, Vol. 14	$ 5	
	B-117	Seeds of Wisdom on the Word Of God, Vol. 15	$ 5	
	B-118	Seeds of Wisdom on Problem Solving, Vol. 16	$ 5	
	B-119	Seeds of Wisdom on Favor, Vol. 17	$ 5	
	B-120	Seeds of Wisdom on Healing, Vol. 18	$ 5	
	B-121	Seeds of Wisdom on Time-Management, Vol. 19	$ 5	
	B-122	Seeds of Wisdom on Your Assignment, Vol. 20	$ 5	
	B-123	Seeds of Wisdom on Financial Breakthrough, Vol. 21	$ 5	
	B-124	Seeds of Wisdom on Enemies, Vol. 22	$ 5	
	B-125	Seeds of Wisdom on Decision-Making, Vol. 23	$ 5	
	B-126	Seeds of Wisdom on Mentorship Vol. 24	$ 5	
	B-127	Seeds of Wisdom on Goal-Setting, Vol. 25	$ 5	
	B-128	Seeds of Wisdom on the Power of Words, Vol. 26	$ 5	
	B-129	The Secret of the Seed	$10	
	B-130	The Uncommon Millionaire, Vol. 1	$10	
	B-131	The Uncommon Father	$10	
	B-132	The Uncommon Mother	$10	
	B-133	The Uncommon Achiever	$10	
	B-134	The Uncommon Armorbearer	$10	
	B-135	The Uncommon Dream, Vol. 1	$10	

□ CASH □ CHECK □ MONEY ORDER

□ CREDIT CARD # □ VISA □ MC □ AMEX

EXPIRATION DATE | | | | | | | | *SORRY NO C.O.D.'s*

SIGNATURE _____

TOTAL PAGES 1, 2, 3	$
SHIPPING ADD 10%-USA/20%-OTHERS	$
CANADA CURRENCY DIFFERENCE ADD 20%	$
TOTAL ENCLOSED	$

PLEASE PRINT

Name _____

Address _____

City _____ State _____ Zip _____

Phone (____) ____ - _____

E-mail _____

Mail to: **The Wisdom Center** • P.O. Box 99 • Denton, TX 76202
1-888-WISDOM-1 (1-888-947-3661) • Website: **thewisdomcenter.cc**

WISDOM 12 PAK

THE MASTER SECRET OF LIFE IS WISDOM
Ignorance Is The Only True Enemy Capable Of Destroying You (Hosea 4:6, Proverbs 11:14)

▸	1.	MY PERSONAL DREAM BOOK	B143	$5.00
▸	2.	THE COVENANT OF FIFTY EIGHT BLESSINGS	B47	$8.00
▸	3.	WISDOM, GOD'S GOLDEN KEY TO SUCCESS	B71	$7.00
▸	4.	SEEDS OF WISDOM ON THE HOLY SPIRIT	B116	$5.00
▸	5.	SEEDS OF WISDOM ON THE SECRET PLACE	B115	$5.00
▸	6.	SEEDS OF WISDOM ON THE WORD OF GOD	B117	$5.00
▸	7.	SEEDS OF WISDOM ON YOUR ASSIGNMENT	B122	$5.00
▸	8.	SEEDS OF WISDOM ON PROBLEM SOLVING	B118	$5.00
▸	9.	101 WISDOM KEYS	B45	$7.00
▸	10.	31 KEYS TO A NEW BEGINNING	B48	$7.00
▸	11.	THE PROVERBS 31 WOMAN	B49	$7.00
▸	12.	31 FACTS ABOUT WISDOM	B46	$7.00

Wisdom Is The Principal Thing

Book Pak
WBL-12 / **$30**
(A $73 Value!)

The Wisdom Center

Money Matters.

This Powerful Video will unleash the Financial Harvest of your lifetime!

▶ 8 Scriptural Reasons You Should Pursue Financial Prosperity

▶ The Secret Prayer Key You Need When Making A Financial Request To God

▶ The Weapon Of Expectation And The 5 Miracles It Unlocks

▶ How To Discern Those Who Qualify To Receive Your Financial Assistance

▶ How To Predict The Miracle Moment God Will Schedule Your Financial Breakthrough

The Secret To 100 Times More.

In this Dynamic Video you will find answers to unleash Financial Flow into your life!

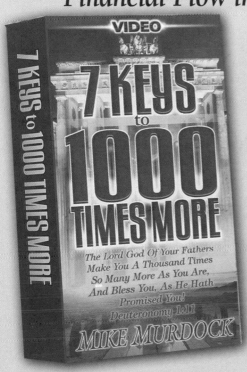

▶ Habits Of Uncommon Achievers

▶ The Greatest Success Law I Ever Discovered

▶ How To Discern Your Place Of Assignment, The Only Place Financial Provision Is Guaranteed

▶ 3 Secret Keys In Solving Problems For Others

▶ How To Become The Next Person To Receive A Raise On Your Job

SOMEBODY'S FUTURE WILL NOT BEGIN UNTIL YOU ENTER.

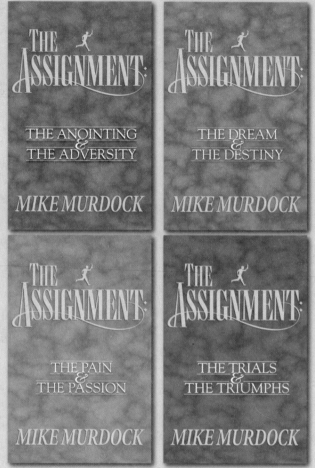

THIS COLLECTION INCLUDES 4 DIFFERENT BOOKS CONTAINING
UNCOMMON WISDOM FOR DISCOVERING YOUR LIFE ASSIGNMENT

▸ How To Achieve A God-Given Dream And Goal

▸ How To Know Who Is Assigned To You

▸ The Purpose And Rewards Of An Enemy

Wisdom Is The Principal Thing

Book Pak
WBL-14 /$30
Buy 3-Get 1 Free
($10 Each/$40 Value!)

The Wisdom Center

Getting Past The Pain.

Wisdom For Crisis Times
Master Keys For Success In Times of Change
Mike Murdock

- ▶ 6 Essential Facts That Must Be Faced When Recovering From Divorce
- ▶ 4 Forces That Guarantee Career Success
- ▶ 3 Ways Crisis Can Help You
- ▶ 4 Reasons You Are Experiencing Opposition To Your Assignment
- ▶ How To Predict The 6 Seasons Of Attack On Your Life
- ▶ 4 Keys That Can Shorten Your Present Season Of Struggle
- ▶ 2 Important Facts You Must Know About Battle & Warfare
- ▶ 6 Weapons Satan Uses To Attack Marriages

Wisdom For Crisis Times will give you the answers to the struggle you are facing now, and any struggle you could ever face. Dr. Murdock presents practical steps to help you walk through your "Seasons of Fire."

- ▶ 96 Wisdom Keys from God's Word will direct you into the success that God intended for your life. This teaching will unlock the door to your personal happiness, peace of mind, fulfillment and success.

Wisdom Is The Principal Thing
Book B-40 / **$9**
Six Audio Tapes TS-69 / **$30**
The Wisdom Center

Learn From
The Greatest.

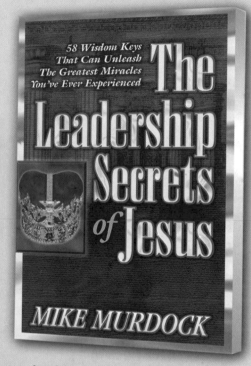

58 Wisdom Keys That Can Unleash The Greatest Miracles You've Ever Experienced

The Leadership Secrets of Jesus

MIKE MURDOCK

▶ The Secret Of Handling Rejection

▶ How To Deal With The Mistakes Of Others

▶ 5 Power Keys For Effective Delegation To Others

▶ The Key To Developing Great Faith

▶ The Greatest Qualities Of Champions

▶ The Secret Of The Wealthy

▶ Four Goal-Setting Techniques

▶ Ten Facts Jesus Taught About Money

In this dynamic and practical guidebook Mike Murdock points you directly to Jesus, the Ultimate Mentor. You'll take just a moment every day to reflect on His life and actions. And when you do, you'll discover all the key skills and traits that Jesus used... the powerful "leadership secrets" that build true, lasting achievement. Explore them. Study them. Put them to work in your own life and your success will be assured!

Wisdom Is The Principal Thing

Book B-91 / $10

The Wisdom Center

Your Rewards In Life Are Determined By The Problems You Solve.

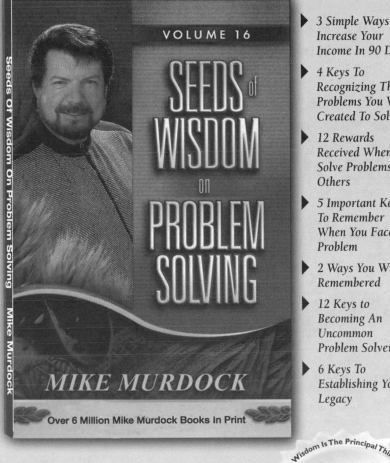

- ▶ 3 Simple Ways To Increase Your Income In 90 Days
- ▶ 4 Keys To Recognizing The Problems You Were Created To Solve
- ▶ 12 Rewards Received When You Solve Problems For Others
- ▶ 5 Important Keys To Remember When You Face A Problem
- ▶ 2 Ways You Will Be Remembered
- ▶ 12 Keys to Becoming An Uncommon Problem Solver
- ▶ 6 Keys To Establishing Your Legacy

Wisdom Is The Principal Thing

Book B-118 / $5

The Wisdom Center

Where You Are Determines What Grows In You.

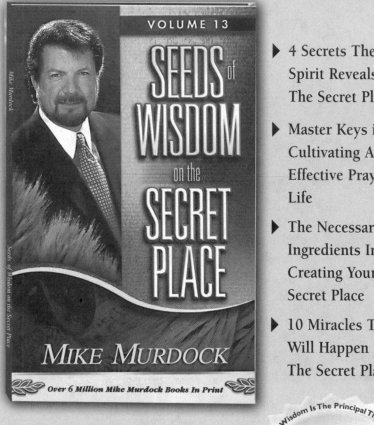

VOLUME 13

SEEDS of WISDOM on the SECRET PLACE

MIKE MURDOCK

Over 6 Million Mike Murdock Books In Print

▶ 4 Secrets The Holy Spirit Reveals In The Secret Place

▶ Master Keys in Cultivating An Effective Prayer Life

▶ The Necessary Ingredients In Creating Your Secret Place

▶ 10 Miracles That Will Happen In The Secret Place

Wisdom Is The Principal Thing

Book B-115 / $5

The Wisdom Center

Run To Win.

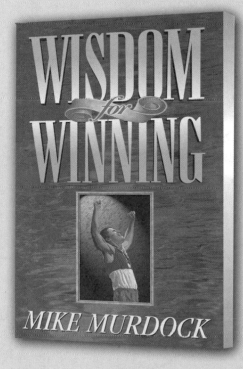

- 10 Ingredients For Success
- Ten Lies Many People Believe About Money
- 20 Keys For Winning At Work
- 20 Keys To A Better Marriage
- 3 Facts Every Parent Should Remember
- 5 Steps Out Of Depression
- The Greatest Wisdom Principle I Ever Learned
- 7 Keys To Answered Prayer
- God's Master Golden Key To Total Success
- The Key To Understanding Life

Everyone needs to feel they have achieved something with their life. When we stop producing, loneliness and laziness will choke all enthusiasm from our living. What would you like to be doing? What are you doing about it? Get started on a project in your life. Start building on your dreams. Resist those who would control and change your personal goals. Get going with this powerful teaching and reach your life goals!

Wisdom Is The Principal Thing
Book B-01 / $10
Six Audio Tapes TS-01 / $30
The Wisdom Center

ORDER TODAY!
www.thewisdomcenter.cc

1-888-WISDOM-1
(1-888-947-3661)

THE WISDOM CENTER • P.O. Box 99 • Denton, Texas 76202

THE WISDOM CENTER

THE SECRET.

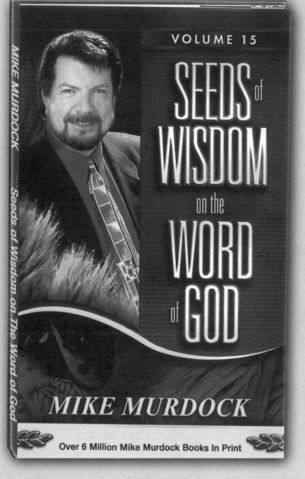

VOLUME 15

SEEDS of
WISDOM
on the
WORD
of GOD

MIKE MURDOCK

Over 6 Million Mike Murdock Books In Print

▶ 11 Reasons Why The Bible Is The Most Important Book On Earth

▶ 12 Problems The Word Of God Can Solve In Your Life

▶ 4 Of My Personal Bible Reading Secrets

▶ 4 Steps To Building A Spiritual Home

▶ 9 Wisdom Keys To Being Successful In Developing The Habit Of Reading The Word Of God

Wisdom Is The Principal Thing

Book B-117 / $5

The Wisdom Center

Your Assignement Is Your Discovery, Not Your Decision.

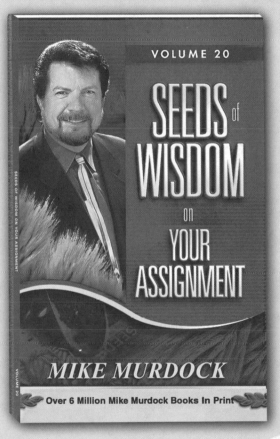

VOLUME 20

SEEDS of WISDOM on YOUR ASSIGNMENT

MIKE MURDOCK

Over 6 Million Mike Murdock Books In Print

▶ 11 Seasons Of Preparation For Your Assignment

▶ 6 Rewards Of Pain

▶ 6 Keys For Developing An Obsession For Your Assignment

▶ 3 Wisdom Keys To Turning Your Anger Into Passion For Your Assignment

Wisdom Is The Principal Thing

Book B-112 / $5

The Wisdom Center

WISDOM COLLECTION 8

SECRETS OF THE UNCOMMON MILLIONAIRE

1. The Uncommon Millionaire Conference Vol. 1 (Six Cassettes)
2. The Uncommon Millionaire Conference Vol. 2 (Six Cassettes)
3. The Uncommon Millionaire Conference Vol. 3 (Six Cassettes)
4. The Uncommon Millionaire Conference Vol. 4 (Six Cassettes)
5. 31 Reasons People Do Not Receive Their Financial Harvest (256 Page Book)
6. Secrets of the Richest Man Who Ever Lived (178 Page Book)
7. 12 Seeds Of Wisdom Books On 12 Topics
8. The Gift Of Wisdom For Leaders Desk Calendar
9. Songs From The Secret Place (Music Cassette)
10. In Honor Of The Holy Spirit (Music Cassette)
11. 365 Memorization Scriptures On The Word Of God (Audio Cassette)

Your Search Is Over.

- ▶ 31 Facts You Sould Know About Problem Solving
- ▶ 21 Keys In Discerning To Whom You Are Assigned
- ▶ 14 Facts You Should Know About Discerning A Golden Connection
- ▶ 8 Facts You Should Know About Wisdom
- ▶ 9 Keys To Successful Negotiations
- ▶ 13 Facts You Should Know About Favor
- ▶ 8 Facts You Should Know About Relationships
- ▶ What Every Winner Must Know About An Enemy
- ▶ What You Should Know About A God-Given Dream

Everything that God created was created to solve a problem. The key to successful living is discovering the purpose for which you were created. This is your "Assignment." Volume 1 on "The Dream & The Destiny" will unleash in you the discovery of your life calling. You will begin to know the joy of being in the center of God's will for your life!

Available also on six tapes for only $30!

Wisdom Is The Principal Thing

Book B-74 / $10

Six Audio Tapes TS-22 / $30

The Wisdom Center